KATHERINE ATWELL HERBERT

THE PERFECT SCREENPLAY

Writing It and Selling It

ALLWORTH PRESS
NEW YORK

10   09   08   07   06   6   5   4   3   2

Published by Allworth Press
An imprint of Allworth Communications, Inc.
10 East 23rd Street, New York, NY 10010

Cover design by Derek Bacchus
Interior design by Mary Belibasakis
Typography by Integra Software Services
Cover photo: © Corbis

ISBN: 1-58115-439-9

Library of Congress Cataloging-in-Publication Data:

Herbert, Katherine Atwell.
    The perfect screenplay/Katherine Atwell Herbert.
        P.   cm.
    Includes index.
1. Motion picture authorship.   2. Motion picture authorship—Marketing.   I. Title.

PN1996.H428 2005
808.2'3—dc22

                                                                              2005035238

Printed in Canada

Dedication

To Stephen Tod, Amy Elizabeth,
and Jill Anne, just because

CONTENTS

Part 1
INTRODUCTION

About Your Self-Confidence

Are you ready? Are you quite sure you're ready? You have to be ready. You have to get yourself ready if you're not already ready. We're talking movies, after all. Screenwriting isn't a right you're entitled to when you reach the city limits of Los Angeles.

If you dream of Hollywood success writing Oscar-winning screenplays, expelling onto paper stories that are giving you brain ache, airing your points of view of life on earth, you've got to be ready to take it on.

You have to get psyched up for the battles that await. You've got to get your mind in the right place to survive.

You've got to be the Jonas Salk of self-confidence and find the elixir that will keep your self-assurance inflated in the face of possible puncturing.

What makes a person ready? Consider the following scenarios:

You've read a couple of books about screenwriting, written a couple of scripts, and perhaps attended a workshop or two held by a brand-name seminar leader. You are feeling pretty good about what you know about the art and craft of screenwriting. You showed your work to your friends, including your great aunt and your mom, because they insisted, and, wow, do they love your work. They tell you it's got success written all over it. Okay, one friend had a little criticism of one of your characters and wasn't too sure how the plot got from point A to point B, but you fixed the one and ignored the other—what does that guy know about writing anyway?

Another possible scenario: You've seen *Adaptation*, written by Charlie Kaufman, and figure you fit the description of the brother. You are not the angst-ridden, sweaty half of the duo whose internal dialogue drowns out all incoming communication. You took a weekend workshop, you're working on your first script—and ohmygod is it a winner or what—you make friends easily and you love to party. Success will find you, of that you are sure.

Or, you are doing an Emily Dickinson. You write in the quiet of your home, maybe you've read one how-to screenwriting book, you hate the thought of scrambling with the madding crowd to actually sell your work, but you know that someday it will all work out. Very soon you will send off your latest script, as anonymously as possible. Some filmmakers will reach out to you across the great divide and pull you into a Hollywood haven where good writers have their material produced without slimy agents or venal producers mucking up the script-to-screen process. Charlie Kaufman probably lives there.

Are the people just described ready? Are you ready? Possibly not. Probably not. Why? Let's discuss.

Person number one is living in a self-imposed critical vacuum. This writer needs to get his or her work looked at with the piercing eyes of a couple of good analysts. No friends or favorite teachers allowed. The writer probably also could benefit from writers' discussion and feedback groups. This doesn't guarantee that the writer will get better, but it can work that way.

Story number two. The pretender doesn't have a clue. Networking and partying are okay as long as there's also some ability, skill, talent even, for writing. Ultimately, as they say, "It has to be on the page." Okay, some "writers" make it not on their talent but on their ability to formulate high-concept, easy-sell ideas. Whatever scripts they attempt are only purchased because a producer sees dollar signs all over the cover and he knows he can hire a real writer to do the rewrite.

Breaking into Hollywood is tough, like scaling K2 without climbing pins. First exception to the rule: You are the wife, husband, son, or daughter of a major Hollywood player—actor, producer, director, and well, you know. Or you are a very close friend, relative, or someone to whom the player owes something. Second exception: You are a certified writing genius. Your work has gained you praise—from more than your mother, notice—and has opened doors for you since you were quite young. Tossing off a bon mot is as effortless for you as clarifying the theories of Wittgenstein and Schrödinger is to a PhD candidate.

SELLING—AN IMPORTANT PART OF THE PROCESS

However, if you aren't connected into the business or a genius, it is going to take effort. You have to be ready for the challenge so you can stay the course until things begin to happen for you. The good news is that you can get ready; you can do it.

The most difficult task you have before you is to make sure your work is salable. Someone has to want to buy it. Hollywood filmmaking is a commercial enterprise. They're in it for the money, and if your screenplay says something important about the human condition or has resonance with the emotions, needs, and desires all *Homo sapiens* share, then so much the better.

The selling part of the effort is the one usually neglected by college teachers, writing mentors, your biggest fans, and others who don't understand the process and naïvely assume that if they consider the screenplay good, then it will get made as soon as a producer somewhere reads it.

With the advent of the Internet and the independent film movement, many writers eschew Hollywood and its brutality and hope to film their scripts themselves or to partner with a friend or a local who is a filmmaker. Nice thought. Rarely works. There's dozens of reasons why, which we will cover later.

Back to Hollywood. The upshot of this naïveté or academia's failure to teach artists how to market themselves—although they have perfectly good reasons for focusing on skill-building rather than selling—is that some young students are convinced they are the next Sam Mendes, or Alexander Payne, Tim Burton, or William Goldman.

To counter this attitude, you should probably conduct a reality check. Whether you admit it or not, thousands and thousands of the people you share the planet with are scribbling scripts. Like you, they also assume they shall one day inherit the mantle of Best Screenwriter.

Unfortunately, there are only two writing Oscars given away each year, so you may not be the one who gets to clean off some shelf space for that statuette. In fact, the field is so competitive that if your work achieves nothing more than getting nice comments from a professional who actually looked at your work, that's an achievement about which you can be proud. Seriously. Succeeding in Hollywood is like winning *Jeopardy*, not *Wheel of Fortune*.

HONING YOUR SKILLS

A second task you must undertake in order to hack out a trail into this profession is to focus on writing skills—learning how to tell stories visually in 120 pages and doing it very well. Once the door on the mailbox swings shut or the "send" button is hit, it's out of your control. There's no chance to fix anything or explain that you plan to fix act two or that after someone buys this version, you'll upgrade to a computer built in the last ten years. It's too late for any of that. The content and the appearance must be in pristine condition before you lick the envelope.

You put this screenplay to paper and disc. That was an arduous job, and you get to pat yourself on the back and buy yourself a gift for completing it. Getting it from your hard drive to the screen at the multiplex, the second half of the process, is your next challenge. It's the part that writers, both newcomers and old pros, have little influence on and hardly any control over at all. And once the opus connects to the U.S. Postal Service and points beyond, self-confidence can slowly seep away.

This book aims to wrest a little of that control and to keep your confidence intact by examining those elements that distinguish a professional script from an amateur one, and to clarify how you can avoid the pitfalls that many scripts stumble into.

So, are you ready? Really ready to take this on? Then let's get on with it.

Your Life as a Writer and the Dish on Operation Hollywood

Art versus commerce isn't a debate as old as time, only as old as maybe the 1920s, when concepts such as "high art" entered the vocabulary in order to make a distinction between popular entertainment, which was a growing cultural force, and serious art. Whether it's valid, genuine, meaningful, or essential to any dialogue about any kind of art and the longevity and significance of that art isn't important here. In fact, it's a discussion that's losing its heat faster than last year's fads.

Noble or urgent intent exists in popular arts as well as the fine arts. So, if you feel you've "stepped down" to write screenplays and that somehow serious writers exist on a more elevated plane, you probably need an outlook adjustment. Otherwise, you won't give your best to your writing and you will never feel good about yourself and what you're doing.

Are there hacks who don't give a damn about anything but producing their by-the-numbers work as fast as possible, whose characters have experiences and emotions that are mostly false and who appeal to the lowest common denominator of human needs and emotions? Sure. Are there writers who don't consider themselves hacks who write formula anyway because they have no deeper understanding of human behavior and emotion than what's generally present in that kind of work? Yes. Does Hollywood pander to the almighty dollar? Probably, but then, the financial stakes are high in Hollywood. Then, too, given the current economy, Hollywood searches for big sellers at the expense of more worthy projects.

IT'S THE QUALITY, NOT THE GENRE

Does there need to be a place where someone who hasn't written a blockbuster script can get produced? Yes, there should be. And probably, as movies grow ever more formulaic and vacuous in pursuit of some mythical audience identified only by demographic charts and graphs, there will emerge also more interesting films that speak to people in the way good films always have. Those films need screenwriters who take their craft seriously.

The move to produce more interesting, complicated, and diverse films may be underway already. Hollywood isn't completely closed to the idea of making films that resonate with an audience for longer than a minute or two after the screen goes dark. By the same token, not all small films are worthy, nor are all films produced outside the purview of Hollywood superior. It doesn't necessarily follow that smaller audiences or the use of subtitles make a film more valuable than one that attracts millions of people and features middle-American speech. *Crash* and

Eternal Sunshine of the Spotless Mind are standard-issue Hollywood films that created hundreds of dinner-party discussions and haven't been forgotten.

All productions—large, small, and in between, independent and otherwise—need to reach a level of professionalism. They need to contain good storytelling and interesting characters, and they have to speak to a truthfulness of human experience before they can expect to touch an audience. Good work comes in many packages.

This isn't a new idea. Throughout history, lots of artists have crossed back and forth between commercial work and projects of their own choosing and have been successful at both. Clear distinctions in the *quality* of the pieces, based on whether they were work for hire or work from the heart, are difficult to make.

Writing copy, creating jingles, or designing graphics with the purpose of selling a product aren't high-minded endeavors. But the *quality* of the work can rival that of the most profound artistic piece—maybe even exceed it.

The line in the sand between art and commerce is becoming less and less distinct when art museums exhibit modern industrial design, fashion designers' work, famous rock-and-roll musicians' instruments, or leather jackets—all commercial products that were designed by commissioned designers.

The importance of paying the rent can never be overestimated. Artists of all stripes might keep their day jobs or take on temporary jobs and only later pursue personal projects, as did photographer Ansel Adams. Now considered the premier landscape photographer, Adams worked for many years shooting pictures for catalogues before ever undertaking his own projects.

Some artists work ordinary jobs during the day but spend nights completing their masterpieces. Colleges and workshops are filled with part-time students who spend their free time pursuing knowledge and skills for the art they want to create.

And some artists may fulfill their talents by creating unforgettable and distinctive magazine covers, advertisements, billboards, or Web sites while hunkering down at their word processors at night, putting together their own novels, screenplays, or graphic pieces.

There are those like Raymond Chandler, a businessman, who began writing what was considered pulp fiction—not a lofty goal at the time—when he was in his mid-forties. He is now considered one of America's best genre novelists, setting the style for such novels and defining the antihero, a character that still predominates in fiction and films.

Conversely, Norman Rockwell, a premier American illustrator whose work continues to speak to the communal experience of Americans and whose work defined the values and experiences of the United States for over twenty years, devalued his immense success and considered himself a failure because he never achieved recognition as a "serious artist" for his oil paintings.

THE SALABILITY ISSUE

You can't ignore the progressive intertwining of commercial and supposedly noncommercial works, or the commercialization of what is considered noncommercial work. It is well known that in today's art world, artists spend a great deal of time "positioning" their work, knowing that the more successfully one can be promoted, advertised, and talked about, the more valuable their work will become, regardless of its true artistic merit—if a means for evaluating art still exists.

This intertwining of art and commerce also exists for people whose day jobs are creative. For example, a sports announcer or a film critic doesn't consider his work commercial; after all, neither of them is selling hockey sticks or shilling movies. They are *reporting on* games or movies. However, if the news director or editor determines that the announcer is dull and people are tuning out, or that the reviewer isn't sufficiently incisive or witty enough to draw readers to the publication, both professionals may be looking for new jobs because they're not helping the ratings or selling newspapers. So in a sense, they're selling a product. Now, they aren't working for the TV station or for the newspaper's advertising department promoting the newspaper, but their work is their product and it must be salable.

The idea of salability also applies to screenwriters. These scribes put their hearts into writing screenplays hoping that someone will agree that the works have quality and value; that the works speak to an important topic, large or small. But scriptwriters have to recognize that like sports announcers and columnists, their works are also products, and have to attract interest from buyers.

Writers may think their scripts ought to sell because they address important issues or exalt an important idea, but generally movie producers buy scripts they hope will do well at the box office.

That reality presents yet another switchback on the road to screenwriting success. After a writer has convinced a producer to read his or her script, that script must also convince the producer that the work will appeal to the public, or to at least a sizable fraction of it. Otherwise, the producer must see the work as unusual, edgy, profound, or interesting enough that it will be capable of creating at least a minor tsunami of publicity and discussion. This was undoubtedly the hope for *The Truman Show* and *Sideways*. Even if a producer falls in love with a screenplay that is not particularly commercial and doesn't seem to have much hope of being a blockbuster, he or she has to consider seriously the consequences of bringing such a project to the screen.

WHAT'S THE COST?

Film is a costly art, a costly investment, and a costly business. Even the most casual viewing of entertainment news shows or perusal of a newspaper's entertainment or business section reveals that making a movie, even a small movie, can cost more than the monthly budgets of many small states. It takes an investment of $10 million to $200 million plus to get a film ready for the market today. No one, except maybe Bill Gates and Warren Buffet, has this kind of money to lose. One look at the figures and it is pretty certain that no one wants to take on a 105-page script with an incomprehensible story, where there's no discernable structure, and whose characters' emotions ring untrue. In an industry that's an uneasy blend of art and commerce, commerce, for practical reasons, is usually the winner.

So always remember that writing screenplays for movies or television, or whatever other forms this art may take in the future, is a commercial craft—that's for certain. That's not actually a bad thing; almost all writing, maybe even poetry, is commercial at some level. You need to be clear about this before you even type the title of your first screenplay—especially if you're of a mind that movies need more obscure material.

THEY'RE NOT ALL BLOCKBUSTERS

It doesn't mean you tuck your heart away and run off somewhere to learn the magic formula, acquire a ruthless attitude, and go for the bucks. Within the loosely organized business that produces feature films, television shows, movies of the week, and even Webcasting, there are plenty of options and opportunities for writers of all stripes to succeed. *Millions*, *Waking Ned Devine*, and *My Big Fat Greek Wedding* have all hit the box-office jackpot, and each was a low, low-budget independent.

Hardly anyone in Tinseltown ever speaks the word "art" or the phrase "art-house film." These terms are regarded as indicative of an effete or academic sensibility with no connection to how real-life working craftsmen create art, bringing to mind images of artists who are too conscious of being artists to produce anything valid or honest. Yet there are artistic, caring filmmakers who hope their work is something more than a mindless piece of fluff. These pieces may not necessarily be arty, nor are they necessarily profound or important. But these filmmakers are not going for the big-scale formula flicks that so many people think of as Hollywood's exclusive concern.

Miramax, Focus Pictures, Fox Searchlight, and other companies offer their share of smaller-scale pictures that concentrate on something other than formulaic scripts and simplistic characters. Such films as *Vera Drake, Sideways, The Hours, The Sea Inside,* and *The Cooler* fit the description. A big budget and big names underwrote Mel Gibson's *The Passion of the Christ,* which only got made because of his reputation and his personal efforts. A more unlikely film couldn't be imagined in this era. Yet Gibson took on the establishment and wound up with a supersized blockbuster for his trouble, and he tapped an audience whose existence Hollywood apparently wasn't even aware of or didn't acknowledge.

With the cost of producing films decreasing because of cheaper cameras and editing equipment, there are probably as many companies hoping to release interesting, unusual movies on the big, little, or computer screen as there are companies whose release slate includes only the predictable formula films with little to recommend them. The Internet enables writers to contact producers and studios directly. With many places to post script and project ideas, and with contests like Project Greenlight and others, more diverse voices will continue to emerge. Some of those projects and screenplays will eventually be produced and released. Hollywood studios may respond by expanding the number and focus of their internal subdivisions—like publishers' imprints—and increase the diversity of their offerings.

THE GREAT AMERICAN SCREENPLAY

So, if you're inclined to conclude that since this is a commercial enterprise you have to swallow your personal vision and lower your standards, just remember that 99 percent of the movies made, both highbrow and low, require a writer whose craft is well honed. Within the industry, writers acquire reputations that range from thoughtful, intelligent geniuses down to mechanics who churn out exploitative shtick that can only be termed "junk food for the brain." Hollywood distinguishes between critically successful writers and commercially successful writers, but it's possible for both types to make a living.

Getting ready to take on Hollywood requires another reality check.

The screenplay has replaced the great American novel and all other forms of writing as the transport of choice to the world of fame, fortune, and getting up close and personal with glamorous members of the opposite sex.

Here's the reality check: Achieving success as a writer probably won't get you face time in *Entertainment Weekly* or interviewed on E! The public hardly ever hungers for the biographical profile of writers. Creating an image, say, on the order of Hunter S. Thompson or Joe Eszterhas can help, as can hiring a good PR person and hanging out at the right parties and charitable events. Marrying the latest and hottest celebrity-actor might bring you a little interest. But you'll probably never be all that famous. If you consistently write successful films, win an Oscar, write stories that say something, and get old and respectable, you might become "known" and the *New York Times* will give you one of their obituaries when you pass on. So keep in mind that if it's fame you obsess over, writing probably won't satisfy.

It may not be renown you are after. You are probably pursuing writing because you have something you want to say, stories you want to tell, and things you've got to flush out of your head so they'll leave you alone. In that case, you're sentenced to life as a writer, with all of its exciting possibilities and all of its pitfalls.

And if the reality doesn't quite match up to the dream, writing a complete screenplay, refining it, and preparing it for the market is an achievement in itself and can't be taken away from a writer. You've done it; you have it on paper. As a member of the writers' ranks you don't get much spotlight time, but aside from the writer-director, the writer garners the most respect in this business.

THE PROPER FRAME OF MIND

If you don't already possess the following three mindsets, you will have to acquire them. They will help boost you toward your goal of selling scripts and making money at it.

First, you have to believe that the stories taking up storage space in your brain must be told; they must be shared with the public. Your motives—educational, enlightening, entertaining—aren't really pertinent; your overwhelming desire to get your stories into the light of the public is what counts. This is the same need that motivates people to write letters to the editor or write guest commentary. They harbor a tremendous need to express what they've got on their minds about a particular topic. They're convinced their views should be heard and that those views should become part of the dialogue arising from current events. The compelling need to write anything is based on the same desire. For whatever reason, you must want your offerings to become part of the world's conversational, inspirational, intellectual, or entertainment currency.

Second, acquire the mindset of a novice. Being a beginner can be an unexpected advantage. Many tyros are simply blind to the competition. You don't know that you're not the only one in the world who's discovered screenwriting, or a new twist to an old story idea. You don't know how very many others there are interested in winning the same lottery you are after. By believing that the goal is attainable, by refusing to take seriously the fact that there is competition, you probably improve your odds of staying on track until you hit the tape. Being a blind optimist has its place. The young often naturally fall into this category simply because they haven't been around enough to understand how the world works, they've spent their time being praised and nurtured by teachers, and they're beginning a new journey which they assume will be successful.

The third mindset that hopeful screenwriters would do well to cling is to the absolute conviction that they are the best and only writers for the stories they have to tell. Further, it probably helps if writers also believe—whether they admit it or not—that no one can write quite as well as they can.

Hold on tightly to these three states of mind; they will be challenged everyday as you forge your way through the Hollywood jungle looking for your Livingston.

PRACTICAL MASTERY

Mastering the more practical aspects of writing for the movies also helps get you ready. It provides its own comfort and will help sustain your efforts, even when you doubt your own ability, or the competition looks overwhelming, or you wonder whether you would rather watch movies than write them.

The mundane aspects of writing include one essential requirement: literacy. Error-laden scripts are immediately downgraded or rejected. Would you hire an auto mechanic who didn't know the difference between camber, castor, and toe-in? To form compelling stories it's essential for a writer to be proficient with the language. The old saw, "Words are writers' tools," is still true—although it's nice to have spelling and grammar check.

Research skills are also a valuable asset for writers. Even when you focus only on what you know intimately, there will be items and areas of your story that will require research. From a simple clarification of, say, how a bartender might successfully skim profits or how a Wendy's franchise works, to doing detailed research on the life of St. Francis of Assisi or string theory, at some point in your writing, research will be necessary. If you don't have a handle on the subject, whatever it may be, you can insult the intelligence of your audience. Once you do that, you've lost.

Writers who possess the art of using language with a natural grace, rhythm, and richness, or as the Germans say, *sprachgefuhl*, have an advantage. This is probably a talent and perhaps simply cannot be learned. But it's worth the time to try and develop the ability by listening to language, by analyzing how some phrases feel complete and almost musical, by considering how words fit together in sentences that make them either flow or clang along awkwardly, without any internal sound pattern and tempo.

IMPROVE YOUR BUSINESS ACUMEN

To stay the course in the field of screenwriting, not only do you need to accept its commercial heart, possess the proper mindset, and master basic writing skills, you also need an understanding of the business.

Although anyone can now post his work on the Internet, that exposure doesn't necessarily guarantee that anyone will see it. It doesn't mean you've brought your product to the marketplace, sold it, and became part of the business; it's more like you self-published a flyer and gave it away, or drew a picture and showed it to your friends. When the first Brownie cameras became available to the general public, it didn't make everyone who took a snapshot a good photographer, much less a professional photographer. Posting verse on a blog does not a poet make.

The same goes for screenwriters.

What's usually required in the arts is the endorsement of other professionals, and that endorsement takes the form of buyers who recognize your work as worthy of their dollars, and/or agents willing to represent you.

You have to present your work to professionals. It's a challenge. Before cable, television writers and producers were well aware that they had three markets for their ideas and material: CBS, NBC, and ABC. They had to interest and intrigue buyers for the three networks or they didn't get their work aired. With the addition of cable and over-the-air channels, the market has broadened considerably, although many broadcasters have specific, narrow audiences. And the advent of reality shows—whose costs are so favorable in comparison to dramatized material that they may never go away—has drained away precious airtime and reduced opportunities for writers. Despite the expansion, the marketplace for writers is still relatively small.

The feature-film business goes through periods of expansion and contraction. In the mid- to late 1980s, several new companies came on the scene, thanks to Wall Street's investments in entertainment. After several companies produced less than spectacular results, Wall Street turned to new areas. Only a couple of the companies begun at that time survived.

Now, with businesses across the board consolidating, with studios already run by conglomerates whose executives don't necessarily understand moviemaking, and with costs climbing ever higher, Hollywood isn't in a particularly expansive mood and the current box-office results aren't setting any records.

Conversely, if and when digital completely replaces film, moviemaking will be much cheaper to undertake. Without the need for prints made from expensive film stock, that part of the process will also become more economical. With computers creating graphics that substitute for real locations, props, and sometimes even actors, the costs drop even farther. The result of all this will be lesser investment, which equals more ability to produce a variety of materials, none of which cost much and none of which will be expected to gross much. Maybe that will happen, maybe not.

If these technical advancements pan out across the board, independent companies will have a real chance to compete, creating films without everyone having to mortgage the farm. With the Internet and the possibility of delivering product online, independent companies looking for success won't necessarily increase their odds by being located in Los Angeles. They may be able to bypass the studio process entirely, unless, of course, they're looking for the traditional release and exhibition in theaters. This is an exciting prospect, and it will be interesting to see if new technology enables independent films to become an important segment of the industry.

However, even if technology succeeds in changing the way business is done in Hollywood, the companies most able to afford new methods of delivery will be the major studios that currently have a distribution system in place. And again, these companies will want to achieve maximum profit and will most likely offer the same kinds of films they offer now, sometimes vacuous, sometimes profound—very professionally done.

There is one thing you can rely on regardless of the direction Hollywood takes. Your screenplay won't get made if it stays in your desk drawer. You have to get it in front of people who will buy the product you are offering.

GETTING BATTLE-READY

So, what more do you need to be completely battle-ready to win screen space and time for your project? There are a few tips we probably need to cover even though you've probably already read or heard various versions of them.

Your buyers—Hollywood producers—aren't teachers, mentors, or people who have your best interests at heart. They're looking for good product. Their job is often on the line to find it. They don't have the time, and often no inclination, to help you improve your skills. Your writing must be honed to get into the big game. Producers won't buy your script just because you think it covers a topic of importance even if it's in rough condition. They have probably already received three others this week that cover the same issues—maybe more eloquently.

Stick to your goal and keep your goal in mind. With extremely rare exceptions, first scripts almost never get bought—that's why they make headlines in *Variety* when they do. Keep writing. You have another story in you. You will get better the more you write. You need a body of work. Agents want to know that writing isn't just a hobby for you. If you find an agent who likes one of your scripts, that agent wants to know that you're not a one-story pony. Most successful writers have a drawer full of early efforts that were never sold (but get dragged out when one of the writer's scripts becomes a massive, and I mean *massive*, hit). Agents will ask you, "What are you working on now?" And you have to have an answer.

As a freelancer, you have to keep selling yourself. When you meet someone who might be interested in buying your script, or someone who knows someone, or . . . you have to let them know you're good at this writing thing and you know how the business operates. When you get the opportunity to pitch a project to an agent, a story executive, or a producer, you have to sell yourself.

You have to present yourself attractively (brush your teeth, put on a clean shirt), confidently, and professionally. The producer wants to know that you know what you're doing, that you can do it within the framework required (time and budget constraints, etc.), that you can see it through to completion, and that you won't cause a multitude of problems for him or her.

Then too, you have to keep at it, keep trying to sell your stuff. You must keep howling at the door. You really have to dog it. You can't let your agent do it, at least not until you're so well established that the agent doesn't have a problem selling you. Make yourself known to people, stop one click short of being an irritant, but be ready, be willing, be available, and keep at it.

NETWORK

Keep abreast of what's going on in the business. You can find out a lot of stuff if you work at a job in the industry, network, keep in touch with people you've met, and hang out with them. You also want to keep up with the daily newssheet—online or paper copies. *The Hollywood Reporter* and *Variety* both report on the daily events of the industry. You'll learn who just bought a major agency or production company, who has signed to star in the next major film project, and the like. More importantly, something you read there may hold a possibility for your career.

Hanging out with people in the business is also an advantage. They all talk about their jobs, and through them you learn a little more about how the business works. Take some classes, and not just writing classes. This is the career choice you made; you need to give yourself as many advantages as you can. You need to know the parameters and specifics of this playground you've chosen to play in.

TOUGHEN UP

You have to learn to take rejection. There's a lot of it in all facets of this business. Most of it isn't personal. You can't let it dissuade you from pursuing your goals. You have to keep on the track you've chosen for yourself. Throw off the inevitable rebuffs and keep going. If it's too painful, you may want to consider another line of work. But really now, why let your dreams die just because one or two people didn't praise your work? The most successful writers around had at least a few editors or producers reject them.

Keep this thought in mind. Do you want your tombstone to say that you had lots of ideas but never got around to putting them on paper? Or do you want your obituary to list all the scripts you've actually written? How do you want to be remembered?

Part 11
ABOUT WRITING THAT SCRIPT

3

Before You Type FADE IN, This May Interest You

It is a little difficult for some writers to admit they are writers.

They hesitate to actually respond to the question, "What do

you do?" with, "I'm a writer." There's something about just

coming out with "I'm a writer" that creates an expectation on

the part of the inquisitor. Depending on the sophistication of

the person asking, many people rather expect the writer to

have written a bestseller or to be working on one. The more

mundane reality, "I write advertising copy," or "I work at the

newspaper," or "I write tech manuals," often disappoints and

terminates the conversation immediately.

WRITING: THE OCCUPATIONAL HAZARDS

Admitting you are a writer can result in a mix of responses, but in our movie- and TV-dominated culture, scriptwriters are almost guaranteed to hear at least a couple of responses if they admit what they do.

The first is, "You ought to write a television series about my job." It doesn't matter what they do. They can work for Google or a government office, in a fast-food restaurant or a video-rental store. Many people assume, except maybe accountants, that hysterically funny things happen at their jobs and that their occupational triumphs and trials are sitcom-worthy. Maybe these people hope for a little understanding from the world—especially if they work in a service job—about the battles they face every day, or maybe they just want their career choice to be the center of attention for a half an hour every week.

A second response screenwriters might get if they reveal their occupation is a variation of, "I have some ideas you should write about," as if writers stand at the freeway entry with a sign: "Will Work for Ideas." Writers who are not permanently or temporarily written out have lots of ideas. They just keep bubbling to the surface like some mental lava pit. Another response you get when you reveal you're a writer is, "I've got a couple of ideas I want to write when I can find the time." Don't worry about future competition from these people—the truth is, they will never put pen to paper.

Writers face an occupational handicap. Because we communicate with the spoken word, many people, especially people who got good grades in high school English, presume they can write and would, if they had the time. Only by having a bestseller on their résumé do writers avoid people who assume they are equals when it comes to putting words on paper. Imagine if our world were mathematically oriented and our common communication transpired via numbers rather than words. Then writing and using the English language would have the hint of mystery and the arcane that numbers now enjoy.

Let's face it, if you're a mathematician or a physicist, no one you meet on the street assumes that if he only had the time he too could develop a unified theory or explain the particle-wave conundrum. But practically everyone, at least within the limits of Los Angeles county, is certain that she's got the next Best Screenplay Academy Award winner percolating in her imagination, just waiting for the day to arrive when she has the time to jot it down.

Real writers don't wait for the day to arrive when they have time. Taking action after you get a story idea divides the nonwriters from the writers. Nonwriters do nothing with their inspirations. Now and then they let their imagination play around with their ideas. In their fantasies, the story tells itself, and they convince themselves that this idea will translate directly to the page when they have time to tap it out on the keyboard.

What these nonwriters know instinctively, but don't reckon with, is that putting the beast on paper reveals all its flaws, its misshapen form, its lack of the essential elements of a screenplay. Translating mental mirages into solid stories is the tough part, the part that makes a person a writer. The nonwriters won't ever put themselves through that brain-melting exercise—it's too much trouble. And it's too scary—their story may not be any good at all. People might laugh. Producers might reject it. They might have to rethink their whole life plan. Meanwhile, the fantasy gives them the hope that one day they will be more than the poor slugs they are now; someday they will rise above the mundane and be rich and famous and thin. There's no harm in daydreams to get you through the rough patches in life, and such imaginings are safer and cheaper than drugs.

You, however, are not in the above category. The lack of commitment doesn't apply to you. You have already passed that demarcation point. You're ready to write. You've scheduled it into your life. And so you begin.

PREMISES

That tugging, nagging sensation at the edge of your consciousness, that insight about life that you had last week, that "What if?" question you asked last night, is beginning to take shape. There might be something here worth pursuing. What do you do about it? Can it grow from inspiration to screenplay?

You need to test it out. See if it works; see if you can build a 110- to 120-page story on it; see if it has any dramatic potential; see if it has any freshness, uniqueness, or interest. Start by putting your story idea on paper. The raw ore you've been mentally mining, expecting to find gold in, should be put on paper in a few paragraphs. You may also want to write down all the notes you have filed in your head about it. Do it—get it all on the page. Read it over then let it sit a couple of days before rereading it. This initial test of your idea will enable you to discover whether this is something worth working on or, now that it's on the page, whether it's lacking in everything that a good story needs to survive. Some ideas sound terrific to our inner voice but reveal their threadbare selves on paper. Once it becomes words on a page, you will be able to consider more realistically whether the idea works, if you can make it work, if it's good enough to pursue at all, or if you're already bored with it now that it's been let out of your imagination and its feeble, underfed condition is apparent.

Thinking and writing are so inextricably connected that this exercise will reveal whether or not your idea has what it takes to become a screenplay. While it rolls around your brainpan, interrupted by other thoughts, dreams, or trying to remember where you left the car keys, it may sparkle and glow. But putting it on the page strips it bare and exposes whatever it lacks. Conversely, whatever magic the idea possesses will also be revealed.

Putting the idea to paper will give it some weight and substance. If it doesn't, if it practically fades off the page because it's so inconsequential and/or silly, you can drop the whole thing right here and move on to another idea. If the idea stands up to the "writing" test, you can be pretty sure you have something worth writing. The next task is to ask yourself, "What and *who* is the story going to be about? What happens? Why will we care about the character and how will we connect emotionally to him or her? What will we watch on screen?"

Some ideas, while perhaps right for an essay, a novel, or even a stage play, just don't shimmer with screenplay potential. One struggling writer wanted to write a script about a young man who doesn't know what to do with his life; all his possibilities foretell only boredom. He may try to kill himself. What are we going to watch on screen, him thinking deep thoughts? That's a little like watching paint dry. What does he do on screen, sit in a chair for 120 minutes picking his hangnails? Again, drying paint. Do we care about this self-involved young man? Probably not much. He sounds immature and self-indulgent. Now, if it is clear that the young man decides very early on to do something courageous, outrageous, or dangerous to counter, forestall, or escape the promised humdrum of his life, then you have a movie.

There have been successful stories about young men concerned with their futures and whether they will have any meaning or not. *Diner* comes immediately to mind, *About a Boy* is another.

After you've assayed this ore, extract the gold by refining your idea, clarifying it in more specific terms, and zeroing in on the essential story. When you do this, you will be able to express the idea, called the "premise," *in a sentence or two.*

It will keep your story on track. Besides, producers and buyers of scripts usually demand to know what your script is about in as few words as possible.

All screenplays start with the premise. Studios and production companies call them "loglines." A premise is the shorthand version of your story. It includes *who* the story is about and what that character *has to do.* Human characters, or characters that behave as humans, are central to all screenplays and form the first half of your premise.

The second part of the logline explains the task, goal, quest, need, or problem the main character, also referred to as the "hero" or the "protagonist," faces. Most films, highly commercial, high concept or not, operate on this basic structure. Here are a couple of examples of premises: A young woman is estranged from her trashy family and lacks any resources, education, or skills. She seeks self-respect, the respect of her fellow man, and a career, so she takes up professional boxing. And another: Two middle-aged men—one about to be married, one a failed novelist—take a road trip to the wine region of California as a final farewell to the single life. They discover much more about themselves than they bargained for.

Do these examples sound familiar? Of course. The first, *Million Dollar Baby*, was 2004's Academy Award winner for Best Picture, and the other, *Sideways*, was an Academy Award nominee for Best Picture and Best Adapted Screenplay.

Remember: A premise is not the theme of your screenplay. That is entirely different. Think of it this way. You have a coin. On one side is the premise, i.e., a character has something he or she must do. On the flip side of the coin is the theme. This is what the film is really about. It's the insight, the lesson, the truth, the humanizing idea that we're left with when the screen goes dark. *Million Dollar Baby* may really be about the possible price we can pay for our dreams. Or that taking big risks brings with it great elation and the possibility of tragic consequences. Or maybe it's trying to say that artificially sustained life is no life at all. You make the call.

Take that well-wrought premise you have forged from the story ore and pin it to the wall over your writing desk. You will need it like the North Star to keep you on a clear path to your story's destination.

After you have it where you want it, take the premise out and drive it around a little. See what other people think of it. Watch their reactions as you tell them your idea. Let other people add their two cents' worth. You don't have to use any of their suggestions, but what they say might give you some ideas about how to develop your screenplay. Just one proviso: Don't discuss your new idea too excessively. You don't want to risk talking it to death.

Test out the premise by comparing it to the films playing at the theaters in your town. Do you have an idea for a movie whose story is inspired by the latest video game, one about otherworldly events, the dead, or machinery that transports characters to some netherworld? Ummm . . . where have we seen that before? How about a story in which a superhero, or a group of superheroes, saves someone or something? Another ummm. You need to get out more—out of the theater, out from in front of your video games, out from in front of the TV.

When Hollywood script analysts read such material, they label it derivative because it is derived not from real life experiences, but from other movies, TV shows, games, or Internet material. It's not fresh, it's not new, and the reader has read stuff just like it a hundred times.

RESEARCH

There's one more step you should take before you begin the actual screenplay: research.

If you are writing about an historic event, place, or person, you'll need to do your research up front. Otherwise you won't have enough information about the era or the subject.

If you are writing something contemporary, once you get the expanded treatment finished you will realize what you need to research. Although you move through the world each day and "know" it, each profession or job has different responsibilities, requirements, conditions, and language and slang particular to it. If your story revolves around two garbagemen, you'd better do some research to see how they work, what drives them crazy at work, what their goals are each morning when they begin their rounds, what conditions prevail in their world, what "terms of art" they employ in the field of waste management, and what slang they use. If you story features a television newsman, get to know a little about how that profession works. You've got to see it from the inside. If an important historical event takes place during your story or a nationally important event has influenced your characters, you'll want to refresh your knowledge of it.

Research is also necessary for specific props and other elements in your script. If you have materials that are important in your script, you'd better know the properties of those materials. For example, do you have a character in your script who is going to escape from a building on nylon thread? Would it hold him? Would it cut his hands to pieces? Could it possibly work at all? You as the writer need to know that. You can stretch reality, you can create a new material, but you should know how the real materials and the real world work—you can't break the rules of the physical universe, so you should know them. Then, especially if you're writing a cartoon or fantasy piece, stretch the bejeebas out of reality.

Another example: If your story involves young children or groups of people you don't encounter every day, again, you need to do research into how their lives are lived, how they speak, what concerns them.

One writer had a script that included the crash of a small private jet. She interviewed an employee of the National Transportation Safety Board to learn step-by-step how that agency conducts its investigations. She also wanted to get a look at the Safety Board's office. She needed to know something about basic aerodynamics and generally how planes behave in crashes. It helped her create a truer picture for those scenes in her story. This sort of research will strengthen your screenplay.

Researching also applies to characters. If you feature a character that has a distinct vernacular or accent, or speaks with a combination of English and a language native to that character, find a real-life example of your character's speech. Listen and take notes. Good research endows your story with a truer feel, and your screenplay will garner better reactions from all who read it.

4

Presto!
Caterpillar Becomes Butterfly

Nothing happens in Hollywood without screenplays. Without them there is no need for anything—repeat, anything—else. No agents or lawyers to negotiate contracts, no actors to memorize lines, no directors, no lighting crews or art directors, no nothing! To quote a famous passage, "In the beginning was the word." In the motion-picture business, it all begins with the words, those found on the pages of a screenplay.

Successful Hollywood screenwriting is about storytelling. There are other kinds of scriptwriting—educational films, nonlinear art films, documentaries, advertising—but the currency of Hollywood is the narrative. If you want to write a good, salable Hollywood script, storytelling is the key.

There are no hard-and-fast rules for telling stories via screenplays but there are some basic texts that are referenced again and again by writers to aid the process. These include the following:

GEORGES POLTI

In 1868—yes, that long ago—a professor by the name of Georges Polti made an extensive survey of literature and came to the conclusion that all story plots fit one of thirty-six models. Essentially, what he did was extrapolate the archetypal pattern of all the stories he surveyed and codify them in his book. In a word, he created the boilerplate. He wrote a book, entitled *The Thirty-Six Dramatic Situations*, detailing his work. He delineates the thirty-six possible story types and the elements that are necessary to successfully create each kind of story. For example, he has one category entitled "Revolt." The essential elements in this story type are a tyrant and a conspirator. But there are additional elements and possibilities for that particular archetype. The story can feature a conspiracy by one individual or by a group of people. Think of *Hamlet* or even *The First Wives Club*.

Not only does Polti cover the gamut of story situations, if you get in trouble, his work can also serve as a guide by providing a discussion of the fundamentals you perhaps forgot to include. Or he can furnish inspiration for turning an idea into a real story by providing the necessary elements to include (for that story type) as you develop your premise.

LAJOS EGRI

Advice written over sixty years ago by a Hungarian playwright who penned his first drama at ten years of age is still sought out by hopeful screenwriters. In 1942, Lajos Egri, who had moved to New York City and taught writing, published a book. Four years later, the book was reworked and became *The Art of Dramatic Writing*. Although the book uses plays as the basis for its discussions on structure, character, conflict, and other topics, his advice applies equally well to film. Later in his career, in fact, Egri left New York and settled in Los Angeles to work in film. Although his advice is not sought as often as it once was, this seminal work can be very helpful to new writers hoping to understand the intricacies of creating a narrative for the screen. Section III of Egri's book, "Conflict," will be especially helpful for creating the structure of your screenplay.

JOSEPH CAMPBELL

If you're writing screenplays, you ought to know something of Joseph Campbell's work, *The Hero with a Thousand Faces*. In case you're unfamiliar with Campbell, he was a professor of comparative religion who became the president of the American Society for the Study of Religion. Campbell wrote many, many books, including *The Power of Myth* and *The Masks of God*. Most of his work dealt primarily with myth and the important role it plays—and always has played—in our lives, spiritual needs, and development.

Through his work, Campbell gained a certain following beyond the academic community, and after he appeared on Bill Moyers's *World of Ideas* on PBS discussing his work and views of man and myth, he became a household word and his writings were included on many people's "must read" lists. George Lucas discovered Campbell early on and invited Moyers and Campbell to videotape some of the episodes of the PBS series at Lucas's Skywalker Ranch.

A student at the University of Southern California and a script analyst, Chris Vogel, also discovered Campbell's work. Campbell's explanation of the hero's journey was to Vogel a template of the underlying story pattern of hundreds of stories and screenplays he had read.

He was so captivated by the material that he wrote a memo to himself about the pattern and the many screenplays that seemed to fall within its parameters. He eventually shared the memo with his coworkers and bosses, and it became known around town. Eventually he expanded on the material and wrote a book, *The Writer's Journey*. It's a storytelling aid for writers that explains in detail the twelve steps of the hero's journey and how they work as the underlying structure in screenplays. Think of *Hotel Rwanda* or dozens of other films. The most notable example is the original *Star Wars*. Vogel describes how movies work in terms of the twelve steps, beginning with a seemingly ordinary hero-protagonist who, like Luke Skywalker, gets the call to action that he must respond to, and thereby begins an adventure full of danger, risk taking, heroism, and finally conquest of the forces that he is battling. Afterward he returns home a changed man.

If the hero's journey approach sounds too involved and overwhelming to you, all is not lost. It's not required that you read the book and follow the steps as if you were painting by number. It wasn't Vogel's goal when he wrote the book. It's also not required that you toss out every plot idea you have if it doesn't seem to follow the pattern. What it does mean is that if you want to be a professional Hollywood writer, you ought to be familiar with the material, the concepts, and at least Campbell's and Vogel's names—even if you're just hoping to *sound* knowledgeable at the next party you attend.

The hero's journey is another way to look at story building. You can see it as a second method, following Polti's thirty-six situations, or you can see how a Polti situation can follow the hero's journey pattern.

ARISTOTLE

Yes, *that* Aristotle. That Greek guy of so, so long ago had opinions on everything, including drama and storytelling. In *The Poetics* he articulated the basic conventions of storytelling, which have influenced writers throughout the ages and continue to do so even in our own time.

Aristotle created the concept that drama must adhere to the unities of time, space, and action. Further, he concluded that drama is required to have a beginning, middle, and end, and spoke of catharsis as one of the purposes of drama. In Hollywood terms, stories have three acts and the feeling that a just and satisfying conclusion is reached by the end. If you're unfamiliar with this concept, it's another one you should get to know. Any screenwriting manual will cover it, and most analysts in Hollywood use it as a basic tool when evaluating scripts. Essentially, the three-act structure consists of the story setup, the complications and development, and the resolution, i.e., acts one, two, and three.

Aristotle's work can be a great help to you as you move from premise to screenplay, which will be discussed in a later chapter. Meanwhile, get your idea on paper before it slips away.

OTHER ITEMS TO MEMORIZE

Remember always and forever that stories are about people, whether your lead character resembles Tom Cruise, Diane Keaton, Bambi, C-3PO, E.T., or the Fantastic Four. If your protagonist is a deer or a chicken, she must behave like a person; she must possess human characteristics and emotion. It can't be said too often: Your audience must connect emotionally to your characters, and they can't get involved if they don't perceive the hero experiencing any human feelings.

The second essential element of stories that you mustn't ignore is conflict. Don't forget the old rule that all stories boil down to one of three kinds of conflicts: man versus man, man versus nature, or man versus himself. And maybe, for the movie world, we ought to include man versus the supernatural or alien. If your characters skate through their lives without encountering any difficulties, resistance, or counterforces—physical, psychological, or spiritual—the audience will keep waiting for the story to begin.

There's a secondary element you want to keep in mind to help give your story some urgency. Oftentimes films put a deadline on events. The wedding preparations have to be ready on time, the money has to be paid by a certain date, the big test has to be taken in three days, or the plane has to be built and flyable by the company's or government's deadline. A due date can be a useful structural tool.

There's also another form of a deadline. The hero has to dismantle a bomb before it explodes, get people out of the path of one of nature's furies, or destroy an asteroid before it hits the earth. In these films, the characters estimate the length of time before the calamity occurs and the plot builds around that deadline. The hero fights not so much against the clock but against an overwhelming force and its ETA.

OUTLINE AND TREATMENT

Your premise has become a gleaming jewel of an idea and you've got some expert direction for structuring the story. Now it is ready to become a screenplay. Before typing FADE IN, however, you should create some guideposts that will lead you from beginning to end. It will be easier if you know where you plan to drive your story.

Begin building the posts by listing every scene you've played in your head, every idea you've had for a scene, every shot you've imagined, and every character you've heard yapping at you. Some of these will be duplicates of the material you wrote before forming your premise. Keep your premise and the list close at hand. Using this material, you are going to create the basic story of your screenplay.

This can be a painful step because it is part inspiration and part analysis. It is here that you have to force yourself to think through the story logically. You will find it is much easier to flip on the TV and see what episode of *Law & Order* is rerunning than face sorting out of your story.

Take the scenes and arrange them in a rational, natural order. When you do this, you will see if there's any flow to the events or if it's a jumble. If it has no cohesiveness, you will need to add ideas. Again, determine what's missing. Add scenes that will tie events together so that one leads to another. Play with them, move them around, drop scenes that don't work. When you have developed an acceptable flow of action, put your ideas on paper. When you are done, you should have a rough outline of your story. By working out the story, you will see if your idea has the seeds to grow into a full-length screenplay. If you try and try but can't get this listing of scenes and ideas to go anywhere, you can drop it, make more modifications, or set it aside for awhile.

If it has potential, then move to the next step. Since you have made some determinations about where this story is going, take your preliminary outline and write a five or more page narrative based on it. As you complete the pages you will gain more clarity about your first masterpiece. When you finish this exercise, read the pages several times. Get the feel of the story. Make sure it flows like a story. Add scenes if things seem to jump around or it seems that things "just happen."

Read the pages to friends and relatives. Get their responses. Don't be afraid. Responses can be very helpful. Set some boundaries to their critiques. Tell them they can't tell you to become an insurance salesman, but they can make comments on the quality of the treatment. Your listeners will be kind. Insist that they tell you if they don't understand something, or if they are confused by the story. They may tentatively ask a question or two. That's good. Listeners will usually bring up lots of things you may not have thought of because you were so thoroughly inside the idea that you missed the obvious. Listen, don't talk in these sessions. Don't justify every little thing you have written and don't get defensive. If you do, your friends will stop helping and you won't get any better.

By completing this treatment you have actually taken a major step toward writing the screenplay. You have done a lot of the actual creative work. Now you need to see to your protagonist.

5

Who's Leading This Trek?
Creating Your Adam

Stories are about people. People go to the movies to see stories of people solving problems or fulfilling a need or under-taking a quest. Feature films, television movies of the week, and TV series are about people. If they weren't, we wouldn't watch them. Even in science fiction, cartoons, and video game–inspired stories, the characters must behave in ways we recognize as human, or the meaning of the stories and our interest in and emotional connection to them will not develop.

Character, then, is the essence of storytelling. All stories are driven by a central hero or protagonist, and the audience must be able to relate to that character. Occasionally movies are made about a group of people, such as *Closer* or *Crash*, but even in these movies, one character usually takes prominence, and it is his or her story on which we focus. There are times in buddy movies that the two characters are equally sympathetic. In *The First Wives Club*, each member of the threesome is equally engaging and draws us to her plight.

Your next step is to create a central character, the hero who can fulfill the promise of your treatment, who is up to the task of running your story.

Your main character, hero, protagonist—all three terms apply—is your screenplay's centerpiece, the engine that drives the plot forward and is in turn driven by the plot's events. The action that this character decides to take after experiencing an event (the inciting or catalyst incident) launches and defines the story. That decision is the "turning point," or "climax," of act one. In *Hotel Rwanda*, Paul Rusesabagina (Don Cheadle) sees the murder and destruction occurring around him and decides he must not flee, but remain in order to maintain the hotel and provide a sanctuary of sorts for Tutsi refugees.

THE QUESTION

Every screenplay raises a question, and how the hero decides to answer it determines what story will be told. In *Hotel Rwanda*, the violence comes close to the hotel early in act one. It might be a story of escape. Can Paul and his family get out of the country safely? It might be a political story. Will Paul take charge and become a leader in the country? It might be a militia story. Will Paul form a ragtag army that makes the hotel over into a fortress and battles all comers? Character is central to the question.

THE CHARACTER ARC

How the character answers the question raised by the plot also forms the character arc. Whatever choice he makes, it will result in a pattern that resembles trekking to the top of a hill. Each step the hero takes is a challenge and takes effort to complete. When the hero finally reaches the top, the climax of the story, he succeeds in answering the narrative question. The trials—the increasing difficult (steep) actions that the hero must undertake—and the events that happen to him gradually reshape his character; your hero should end a story as a slightly or profoundly different person because of them. Hence, the character's arc from one state to another.

BE REAL

There's a lot riding on the protagonist, so it's important that this character be well developed and have what is referred to as "felt life." The audience has to believe this person has the full range of emotions, the frailties, the virtues, the needs, and the gifts as do the people we interact with every day. Back to our example: Paul experiences great fear and displays bravado, tenderness, wiliness, compassion, pride, disappointment, and various other emotions. We can read them all on screen. And while an actor can bring a character to life, the descriptions, the personality, and the characterization of the role has to be on the page in order to guide the actor's interpretation.

People live interior lives behind the image they present to others. There are qualities about the people around us that we are unaware of. Characters in screenplays, especially the protagonist, should be endowed with an implied private self. The best actors bring a character's internal dimension to the fore. Think of some of the work of Sean Penn or Keifer Sutherland or Cate Blanchett. When we watch them, we know their characters have thoughts and emotions that bubble under the surface and that make them much more interesting. Only the most immature or shallow writer is satisfied with creating a flat, surface-only character, although these characters sometimes work for cartoonlike action or animated movies. Often the female love interest in these films is one-dimensional. Even in these instances, however, the screenplay is enriched if the characters are full-blown people.

BIOGRAPHY

One proven method for capturing your main characters on paper is to write a biography for each of them. The biographies should include the facts of the characters' lives, physical descriptions, their particular worldviews, their attitudes, the pains and pleasures they've experienced in their lives, their fears, habits, and virtues, and their current concerns.

"Back story" refers to everything that happened, before page one or the opening scene, that's pertinent to the story. Your characters have back stories, i.e., a past. The audience must feel that these characters have ongoing lives that began before page one and will continue after the end credits. In the screenplay, you need to include the elements of your characters' back stories that are important to the story or help reveal their characters.

The biography will enable you to keep your character behaving consistently and avoiding abrupt and unbelievable changes included only to make the plot work.

Twisting around a character's personality to fit the needs of the plot is a weakness often seen in television series characters. To make the episode's plot work sometimes requires the character to behave quite differently in different episodes. Even a show as well turned out as *Monk* sometimes falters in this respect. For although Monk, with his many phobias, is constantly challenged to face those fears and is forced into action in order to save the day or solve the crime, there have been episodes in which the degree of his fear is greatly changed from previous episodes; then it will switch back again. Then, too, the police department seems to go back and forth. In some episodes, Monk is "da man" to turn to, while in others, they only reluctantly call on him for his expertise.

NEEDS

Building in the very qualities the hero will need to prevail against the antagonist is a must for creating a believable character. Whatever quality, skill, or knowledge will be needed by the main character to solve his/her problem should be included in the biography. For example, usually in act one the hero will do something that indicates he possesses a particular quality, skill, or knowledge. Once established, the audience isn't surprised when in act three the hero employs that quality to win the day. A simple and often-used quality is the willingness to take risks. In act one, the hero does something risky, like, say, driving on the wrong side of the street in order to win a street race, disobeying department policy, or defying a teacher for a good cause. This establishes the character as a person who is willing to take risks when the need arises. Later, in acts two and three, this quality will be required if the hero is to win the battle.

TEST YOURSELF

Here's a short exercise that might help you gain more insight into your character:

1. What is the worst thing that ever happened to your character during his/her childhood?

2. What aspect of your character's appearance most troubles him/her, or what would he/she most want to change about that appearance?

3. What's the one thing you character knows about himself or herself that he/she wouldn't want revealed publicly?

4. What is your character's favorite kind of entertainment?

5. What is your character's greatest weakness?

6. What issue sets off your character?

7. What does you character need more than anything else?

8. Has your character ever had his/her heart broken?

9. What's the worst thing your character has done and gotten away with?

10. What's your character's most annoying or unconscious habit?

Once started on this exercise, you will probably think of more questions to ask about your hero.

You want to create a fully human protagonist. But heroes also follow the conventions established by commercial Hollywood films, so you might want to keep in mind the following items.

STEAL FROM LIFE

As detailed earlier, your characters must strike the reader as real and true to life; analysts need to feel the character could actually exist. One way to ensure this is to steal from the people you know. Characters based on real people assure a truer depiction.

When you base your characters on people you have known, or on an amalgam of different people you have known, you'll avoid creating stereotypical characters. Stereotypes are the bane of Hollywood development people. These characters have no personality, no individuality. Stereotypes are abstractions of groups that society or sociologists or the media have labeled in a particular fashion. They include the spoiled rich boy, Neanderthal thugs, vicious mob bosses, redneck bigots, poor white trash, grandmas, blondes, etc. Avoid writing types, even in your minor characters. Although we may all match parts of a stereotypical pattern, no one is so lacking in individual needs and quirks that she is nothing more than the sum total of a stereotypical abstraction.

Occasionally a character who has no dialogue serves only as a functionary, e.g., waiter, maid, cashier. There is no need to describe these characters or give them names. But any character who has dialogue and appears in even one or two small scenes should be given at least a little personality.

Children are difficult to write. People who aren't around them, and even some who are, often reveal their ignorance of children when they create characters under eighteen. One script I analyzed revolved around a six-year-old. In one scene, the child was coloring and making a mess of his mother's room; in the next, he was advising an adult character, spelling words, and dunking a basketball.

If you don't have a child or aren't around a child the age of your story's character, then you need to do some research. Watch children. See what levels of maturity they generally exhibit at various ages. Find out how evolved their psychomotor skills are at different ages. Listen to their vocabulary. Don't assume that just because the children you have seen on TV are intellectually, socially, or sexually sophisticated, all children are. Children in sitcoms are notoriously unrealistic, included only to serve the plot.

Don't make assumptions about the behavior of children from socioeconomic levels, races, or ethnic groups different from your own. (Don't do it with adult characters either.) If you're writing a child into your script, find out what the real-life varieties are like.

Here's the secret exception to the suggestion that realistic characters are the ideal. Movie people aren't really duplicates of the real people you bump into every day. Although they must appear to be real people, they are only real within the context of the story. As with almost everything in the movies, reality is pushed a bit. Harrison Ford may be presented as an ordinary guy in *Witness*, but he's actually a little bigger than life. Real guys don't use their fists, their wit, their inner resources, their physical prowess, or their charm with such regularity or with quite the same high rate of success as movie heroes do.

KEEP IT COMPLEX

The most interesting characters in screenplays are those who are the most complex. Their personalities can't be summed up in a word or two. They have their own quirks, their own ways of approaching life, from talking to a clerk in a store to talking to the President, from putting on their clothes to washing their face to walking down a hallway. From their views on life to their opinions of events around them, your characters, and most assuredly your protagonist, should exhibit some texture and layering that will prevent the audience from knowing everything about them at the end of page one. They will be revealed as the story progresses, just as occurs in real life.

WORDS SOMETIMES SPEAK LOUDER THAN ACTIONS

Once you've gotten a clear understanding of your protagonist, you must make sure that his or her speech and conversational style is consistent with the personality you've created. The character's behavior and actions must also work in harmony with his given personality. A simple example: If you've described a highly nervous, agitated person, it's unlikely that she would stroll slowly or stay calm in a crisis. And think what coffee would do to her.

MOTIVATION

If you've got your protagonist and the other major characters clearly delineated, you've completed an important step. Now, you've got to supply them with adequate motivation. In your story, the protagonist is going to be faced with a problem he or she must resolve. The reader must understand why the hero keeps fighting through this crisis. In *Hitch* the motivation is clear and quite simple. Hitch (Will Smith) has to protect his business and he doesn't want to lose the woman he's fallen in love with. In *Kinsey,* the sex researcher (Liam Neeson) feels strongly that he will help his fellow man by bringing discussions of sexuality into the open and providing valid, scientific information on the mechanics of sex, our attitudes about it, and how our needs are manifested.

JUST FOR THE PASSION OF IT

The viewer also has to believe that the protagonist has an investment in the outcome of the problem—otherwise, why would he get involved? If there is no investment, if the hero isn't passionate about the quest, the audience won't care if he is successful. The audience also has to believe that the conflict or problem itself is important and worth the hero's time and trouble.

The thing to avoid like the West Nile virus is a passive hero. No one wants to see the hero sit around waiting for things to happen to him. The hero has to take charge, take action, and take us with him.

CONSISTENTLY HUMAN

Here's another one of the curves that's thrown at writers. While story editors and analysts tell you that characters need to behave in accordance with the personality they've been given, analysts still want to meet characters who surprise them.

They don't want characters who are too boringly consistent, because that isn't realistic or interesting. In real life, a person may truly believe in a certain principle or mode of behavior but be blind to the fact that he himself violates that principle occasionally. Your protagonist's actions shouldn't contradict the limits of the personality you've assigned him, but sometimes he needs to react to situations in unexpected ways. For example, if your protagonist is a detective who doesn't believe in breaking and entering because it's illegal, then he does it anyway, it can be explained that breaking and entering was the only means possible to obtain some crucial information. Or the hero can charmingly admit that he doesn't take his own pronouncements too seriously. By avoiding stultifyingly consistent behavior, your characters become more interestingly human and endearing to an audience.

CONNECTING EMOTIONALLY TO THE HERO

In most Hollywood films, we sympathize with the hero. Although there are those filmmakers who hate this formulaic approach and insist that audiences will come to see movies that feature complex but not necessarily sympathetic characters, the majority of movies released feature a protagonist the audience can root for. It doesn't mean your lead character has to be a Dudley Do-Right or an unblemished all-American hero.

In *Payback*, Porter (Mel Gibson) is a thief. After he and his partner rob a mob courier, his partner shoots him and takes Porter's share of the booty. Porter's world is peopled almost exclusively with double-dealing criminals. So although he too is a "bad" guy, in this setting we sympathize with him and root for him as he tries to retrieve his fair share—$70,000. He wants no more and will settle for no less. The audience winds up sympathizing with a bad guy—albeit a bad guy who isn't as bad as the guys he's battling.

But tread lightly in this area. Hollywood prefers your main character to start as likable and end up being even more likable, although you've taken him through test after test of everything he stands for. In short, you are safer with characters who can engage an analyst's or producer's sympathy.

GETTING STARS OUT OF YOUR EYES AND INTO YOUR MOVIE

We can discuss all the high-minded concepts about character from now till the turn of the next century, but there is a down-to-earth, practical aspect to character. Writing characters we can root for is smart, but even smarter is writing characters that influential actors, otherwise known as box-office draws, will be interested in playing. Actors want to play interesting people, people of action and determination, complex people. They don't want to play stereotypes, passive people who let life run over them, two-dimensional people, or people who have no emotions whatsoever. This applies even to current action films. Think of how much more fun Jackie Chan is than, say, several of the super action heroes who preceded his domination of the box office. Making your protagonist appealing to prominent actors is reason enough for developing the best character you're capable of creating. There are actors in Hollywood who can get movies made.

SHOW US, DON'T TELL US

When you finish creating your protagonist and the characters that surround him, and you are sure you understand them inside and out, you've got to put them on the page and let the reader get to know them.

Analysts and producers prefer that we get to know characters through their actions. We learn more from how a character acts and relates to others than we do through dialogue. And writing a lot of descriptive background for your characters is a way to kill interest in a script and put producers and development people into sleep mode. Not only is it dull, but also it's the least effective way to reveal character. Dialogue is a better approach, and the best way to disclose character is through action and what the character chooses *not* to say. Think of it like this. If you have a line of description that says your hero hates cats, what does that have to do with what we will see on screen? If you have one character say to another, "You know Jimmy [the antagonist] hates cats," then we know something about Jimmy, but so what? Conversely, if the antagonist comes into a room where a cat brushes up against his pant leg and he kicks the feline across the room, then we know, without a doubt, that he hates cats and what he's capable of doing. And we know from our understanding of story structure that the cat will come back into the picture eventually.

SUMMING UP YOUR LEAD CHARACTER

Characterization, then, is the writer's primary concern. Characters drive the story. It is their actions and their decisions that get them mired in the story's problem. But it's also their personalities and personal qualities that will eventually get them out again.

Some Specifics about the Blueprint and the Interior

Before you warm up the computer and type FADE IN, some

story suggestions and review will help your screenplay remain

on track.

STRUCTURAL GIRDERS

New writers improve their chances of success if they gain a general understanding of the conventions of story structure. This approach to constructing screenplays wasn't invented by Hollywood, so negative associations you might harbor are misplaced. The storytelling template is based on the work of Aristotle and Joseph Campbell, introduced in chapter 4.

The narrative I-beams that undergird most *successful* films follow the same general pattern, whether it's a charming little $80,000 independent offering or a $100,000,000 Hollywood epic, and whether the structure is clockwork or amazingly subtle.

Remembering Aristotle's beginning, middle, and end—and don't underestimate that seemingly simple structure—your task is to take that terrific premise, outline, and treatment you created and build a solid structure to hang your plot on.

Aristotle's beginning, middle, and end can be translated as act one, act two, and act three. This is the structure movies generally follow. It doesn't imply that you must force your material into some Procrustean bed. There's more than ample room to tell a unique story. What it offers is a path that will keep your story from getting lost in a narrative wilderness or disappearing at page forty-five or seventy-three or eighty-nine without an ending. Is every film structured this way? No, of course not. Films such as *Forrest Gump* are a series of individual stories linked together only by the main character. Some screenplays, like *Vertigo* or *Butch Cassidy and the Sundance Kid*, can more logically be divided into two acts. And some, like *Crash* or *Nashville*, while following a loosely conceived beginning, middle, and end, feature several story lines all developing concurrently. Generally, however, three acts have proven to be a successful method of telling a story.

Another element of structure that is recommended for successful storytelling is the through line. The through line is essentially the main plot, the question that is raised and must be answered. That's why it's a through line; this plot line goes *through* the entire story. The primary story is established near the film's beginning and is resolved in the climax of act three. It works as an audience "carrot." The audience remains intrigued by the movie because they want to know how it will turn out, i.e., how that question will be answered. Each of the three acts pushes the story forward in unique ways that keep the through line moving to create the narrative arc.

Writers give themselves a helping hand by understanding the purposes of the acts and determining what major events occur in each. In that way, the writer knows what point he or she must reach before the act is complete, and that provides direction and a goal for the writer. It helps prevent the story from wandering aimlessly—an arch-killer of scripts.

THE ACTS

The boilerplate screenplay is 120 pages long, which translates to two hours of screen time. The standard rule: One page of script roughly equals one minute of screen time. This length is a little long for comedies and high-concept action films and a little short for epics and some heavy dramas, but you will want your screenplay to fall within this time frame. The acts are divided as follows: act one, thirty pages; act two, sixty pages; act three, thirty pages.

Act One

It is in this act that you set up your story by letting us know where we are and what time period we are in, showing the world the characters belong to, introducing your characters, establishing the mood and ambiance of the movie. Act one usually includes some foreshadowing and quickly reveals important character traits the hero possesses, qualities that will be needed later on in the film so the hero can solve the problem he faces.

The primary function of act one is to launch the story. After orienting the audience so they know where they are and what people they will be watching, the writer has to get the main action underway. Act one is completed once the story has begun.

The narrative question is raised in act one. For example, in *Armageddon* the question is: Can the team headed by Bruce Willis's character destroy the asteroid before it crashes into the earth? The question raised by *Pieces of April* is: Can April (Katie Holmes) successfully pull off her first Thanksgiving dinner for her disaffected family? You have to determine the question your screenplay raises. It can be anything that engages an audience or that has enough gravitas to be worth writing about. Saving the earth from asteroids, saving the world from terrorists, saving a classroom full of delinquent students, learning to accept unloving parents, learning to live with loneliness, or discovering that material wealth or acceptance by the "in" crowd isn't all there is to life are all valid topics and have been done many times in different films.

Your job in act one is to set up the story and raise the question. An event has to occur early on that sets the story in motion. This event is usually called the "inciting incident" or the "catalyst event." It forces the protagonist to take action. For example, say the hero has been involved in a robbery. Before he can get away, the police arrive, so he hides the diamond he's stolen in an air vent of the building he just burgled. When he gets out of prison a few years later he goes back to get the jewels, but finds that the building has become the home of the police department. The inciting incident is his decision to hide the jewel in the building.

The question raised by the story is this: How the heck is he going to get into this forbidding place and get his prize? That is his quest, problem, desire, need, and challenge. It is what every hero must have. And, too, the hero has to care deeply about his challenge, and in this film, the thief does. When the hero decides on a particular course of action, that is the climax or the turning point of act one. Now the audience knows whose story we're going to watch, what the hero has to do, and what question will be answered by the story's end. Act one is finished. This is the structural basis of your screenplay.

In this particular screenplay, *Blue Streak*, Miles Logan (Martin Lawrence) tries several strategies before impersonating a policeman in order to gain access to the building.

If you insist that your hero cares very little, that he has no passion, the question that will occur to the audience is: What will happen to the hero that will make him care again? And how will it do that? Paul Newman's character in *The Verdict* was in just this situation. Redemption stories often open with defeated, withdrawn characters. Over the course of the story they come to care and find a reason to hope and engage life.

If the hero, an ordinary happy-go-lucky guy, doesn't care about the question raised, or cares a little, then you've got trouble. Your main character must be compelled by his quest, his problem, his need, or his challenge. If he isn't, then the audience also isn't engaged. Your main character must also be fully committed; he must care deeply about whatever problem confronts him. If he does, then the audience will be his cheering section and will want to see him succeed.

The Fugitive is a textbook example of a very successful film that follows this pattern. The plot focuses on Dr. Kimble, arrested for the murder of his wife, though he insists that a one-armed man committed the crime. His conviction for murder acts as the inciting incident. The climax of act one is an exciting, extremely cinematic train-bus wreck, after which Kimble, who survives, decides to run. He could have stayed to tend to the injured, he could have searched for a phone to call authorities, he could have waited for help to arrive; he was after all, injured himself. If he had made any of those decisions it would have been a very different film. By deciding to become a fugitive, he determines what kind of movie is in store for the audience. The story's question has been raised: Will he manage to outrun the law? The hero's decision is the true climax of act one; that decision defines and launches the story, although adding a big action event like a train wreck punctuates it with pizzazz. Act one is done.

Act Two

That brings us to act two, which is trickier and longer. The template calls for about sixty pages in this section, roughly from page 31 to page 90. The job to get done in this act is developing the plot with all its complications. This section also colors in the characters with their own personalities; the audience needs to get to know them.

In *The Fugitive* the audience gets to know Kimble a little better. We learn that he's resourceful, determined, and willing to take risks; he can think through problems and arrive at important insights and he doesn't back down from a fight.

The early complications he faces are fairly simple—he has to avoid being caught. When he decides to find the killer himself, the complications and staying out of the hands of the law become tougher. He must find ways to search for the real killer, obtain pertinent information, and follow up on it, all while keeping one step ahead of the U.S. Marshals.

Act two—and again, this is true of *The Fugitive*—often introduces the antagonist for the first time. If the character has been previously introduced, it is in act two that he or she is revealed as the villain, as was the case in *Spider-Man*.

New characters who help or hinder or interact with the protagonist in minor or major ways are introduced and given their own jobs and personalities in this act. Characters who began in the background can come to prominence, and sometimes in act two, a character is added, if he hasn't already been introduced, who will serve as a catalyst for the hero's actions in act three. Jack Black's character in *Orange County* served this function for Colin Hanks, who plays his younger brother and is the story's hero. It is probably not a good idea to introduce a new character, especially an important one, late in act two.

To successfully tackle the second act it can be helpful to divide it into two sections of thirty pages each, ending the first section, the midpoint of the script, with its own mini-climax.

How do you approach all this development and complication? Remember the central role of conflict. Whatever it is that your hero is fighting for must be difficult to achieve—otherwise it isn't worth the heroic effort that will be made. For example, you write a screenplay about a young woman who wants to take a journey from Boston to Los Angeles by herself. But if she goes with the good wishes of her parents, has ample money, drives a reliable car, sees a lot of fascinating sights, and has an all-around good time, you have a travelogue, not a screenplay. You don't have conflict or any possibility of dramatic counterforces working against her. You need to go back to your premise. Is it compelling enough to generate any interest for anyone? Who really cares about people taking a trip across country? So many people have already done it and taken their own pictures. Even if your focus is on the weird or the offbeat or just on haunted hotels, you still have a travelogue.

Return for a moment to the premise, outline, and treatment. You need to build in a more critical reason for the woman undertaking the trek. Is she in a wheelchair and needs to prove herself so people will stop patronizing her? Does her estranged mother live on the opposite side of the country and now that she's older or been diagnosed with a disease, she needs to reconnect with her mom? Did her mother make this same trip and the young woman has to do it also in order to discover at which stop along the way, by which of her mother's lovers, she was conceived? Does she have to take some crucial papers to someone but all means of transportation except her car are unavailable to her? There are many other possibilities to reshape the original premise into one that raises a question that must be answered by film's end. Check your treatment. Do the scenes you're writing contain any conflict? Is there any tension promised in them? There should be both. If you don't have both conflict and tension, you will need to rewrite those scenes.

Adding a deadline can up the ante for the young woman crossing the country. Maybe she has to get to L.A. before she misses out on a prize jackpot or before her favorite aunt dies of cancer or before a film producer offers a plumb role to another actress.

When you begin act two, determine what complications will arise and what forces will work against the woman to prevent her from succeeding at her quest. Again, if these counterforces don't exist, then there is no conflict, and hence, no story. If this trip is as easy as going to a fast-food drive-through that gets your order right the first time, then there's no story.

You must plan what events will occur that will make this trip a lighthearted or serious ordeal, and it must challenge her. You must decide what other characters will play a role in her quest. Will her mother move in and out of the story either via phone, meeting the young woman at various points along the way, or by flashbacks? Will her boyfriend or best friend offer help or present problems? Does the boyfriend and/or girlfriend have his or her own story that you want to include?

Say the young woman has to make the trip for the sake of the dying mother she last saw when she was six. Reconnecting with our parents is a recurring theme in movies and stories because our feelings about our parents are so strong that this theme continues to hold interest for audiences. Furthermore, say the girl's car is a real junker but it's her only option. Determine that the boyfriend can't go, for his own selfish reasons, and insists that she cancel her plans. Perhaps the best friend plans to go with her but at the last minute is prevented from doing so for some reason.

Your hero/protagonist/main character has to face problems (and some pleasures) along the way. Structurally the hero usually begins well and efforts are met with success. Before long, though, the little problems that seem harmless become big problems, big conflicts appear, and things in general grow more negative, ominous, and threatening. Success turns to failure. Little successes lead to big failures.

Decisions made by the character don't always work out well—especially in the case of comedies. Forces work on the character that test him or her; the protagonist's own personality influences the kinds of decisions made. Sometimes the hero's moral compass fails and a decision is made that brings more unforeseen complications.

The young woman may have car problems. Her engine starts to miss as act two begins. The young woman ignores it. Near the end of act two, the car breaks down completely. More complications: The woman, previously characterized as very friendly and a little naïve, exchanges innocent greetings with a fellow at a roadside café. Later in act two he catches up with her and tries to rape her or rob her or waylay her in some manner. Conversely, he may be a happy experience. They may fall in love—or they may fall in love until his old girlfriend or her old boyfriend arrives on the scene.

Driving cross-country and facing a continuing series of challenges and pleasures can get monotonous if all the events are too similar in character, tone, seriousness, or length. For example, the young woman can get lost once or twice, but you can't keep falling back on that tactic. Or, if she has car trouble, that can't be the only source of complications. Each successive event should be a little more serious than the previous one, with successes and failures mixed.

As each complication rains down more problems and as the deadline gets closer, things escalate; the woman becomes more stressed and distraught. This is a description of rising action, another essential in good solid story structure. Similar to the character arc, rising action can be diagramed as hill-like.

Avoiding events that are too similar in character, tone, seriousness, or length will help provide a rhythm and pace to the film. Listening to the same drumbeat over and over and over and over grows monotonous and irritating. Given different pitches and tempos and a variety of drums, the percussion not only becomes interesting, but can also become hypnotic and rise to a grand finale—just like you want your screenplay to do.

To avoid a repetitious feel you're going to avoid a series of similar complications. Instead you are going to layer in subplots, continue to develop your main character and perhaps other characters as well, and enrich this straightforward, linear plot with interesting sidebars, surprising turns, and interesting characters who may have their own stories or who at least add some flavoring to the plot. Watch Bronson Pinchot's take on his tiny role in *Beverly Hills Cop* playing a clerk in the art gallery who has a very odd accent. He adds physical flourishes to his character's actions, and his dialogue and timing match Eddie Murphy's (playing Axel Foley) like two stand-up comedians doing a routine. Suddenly this small scene, in which Foley is simply asking where he might find his old friend from Detroit, becomes a memorable, funny bit of fluff instead of a dull segue piece.

Current conventional screenplay structure prescribes that if you are writing a screenplay that has an upbeat ending, then the turning point of act two is downbeat. It will seem to the hero that all is lost; all the efforts to answer the question, achieve the quest, and meet the challenge have failed. In Campbell's twelve steps, the hero at this point in the story has entered the enemy's lair and it doesn't look like he will get out. Luke Skywalker and Hans Solo find themselves in a giant trash compacter about to get crushed and tossed into the vacuum of space. No solution to this overwhelming problem presents itself; their quest will end in failure and death.

In *Million Dollar Baby*, the fighter's injury is the turning point in act two. She's done. The second-act climax of *The Fugitive* is Harrison Ford's discovery of who is actually behind the murder of his wife and the devastating nature of that knowledge.

In the young woman's story, she may be so overwhelmed by all that's happened to her, all the battles she's fought with man, machine, and geography, from page thirty to about seventy-five or eighty, that she is done in, or injured, or no longer believes in herself. All seems hopeless; she will die by the side of the road in Winona, Arizona, and her quest won't be fulfilled. Act two is finished.

Act Three

The final section of the script is called the short, fast act. The task of this section is to resolve the problem once and for all; to reach the final showdown, literally in old Western films and action flicks, but metaphorically otherwise. For the young woman of our example, that may mean one of two things. She can make it to Los Angeles and confront and resolve what has driven her to take the trip, or she can realize that it isn't necessary to succeed at what has become an impossible task. The first instance can reflect the usual "happy" ending; the second is often considered a "down" ending. However, in both cases there's a resolution to the problem and the protagonist has completed the quest; both could be "up" endings.

In act three, the action is at its peak of urgency and tension. Everything is at stake. The hero is betting it all on this final, crucial battle. It is all or nothing. In *The Fugitive*, act three is essentially a chase, which is true of many action films. The federal marshals chase Kimble as Kimble chases and battles, hand-to-hand, man-to-man, the person responsible for the murder of his wife. The climax of the film, which takes place at the end of this fast act, resolves the question raised by the film. It is the catharsis, mentioned earlier in the book, a concept that's been around since the Greeks. Part of the purpose of those ancient Athenian plays was for the audience to feel the pleasure of the cathartic response—the problems of man and the gods were resolved. For a moment, at least, all was right with the world. Today's movies follow the same model.

Act three generally begins with the hero at a very low point, wondering if the cause is worth fighting for and figuring that his life is finished, forever changed for the worse, and his dream lost. But somehow the defeated character gathers the strength and determination to continue on with the fight, the last chance to achieve the goal. At this moment the catalyst character may reappear. That character can be an encouraging parent, a relative, a best friend, or someone who has been cheering the hero on from the beginning. The person arrives to pep up the protagonist and encourage him or her to continue the battle. Cyn (Joan Cusack) in *Working Girl* is a reluctant catalyst for Tess McGill (Melanie Griffith) to continue her battle to become an investment analyst-manager. In the film *Disclosure*, Tom Sanders (Michael Douglas) has an anonymous friend who contacts him by e-mail and acts as the catalyst, helping him with encouragement and information so he can launch a last stand in his battle to save his career.

In simplistic action films it is often at this turning point that the one-dimensional but gorgeous female character comes in to comfort the hero. She mends his wounds and sees to his physical and psychological needs. Following the tryst, the now-revived hero takes on the enemy for a battle royale.

Act three is urgent. The hero's time and options have expired. This is the act in which the hero finally has a clear picture of what has been happening all along. The hero finally understands what's preventing him from succeeding at his quest, reaching the goal, or meeting the challenge. He gets the true nature of the problem and realizes what must be done about it.

The showdown is the only way to resolve it once and for all. It is usually here, in cleverer films, that the final scheme is put into action, little of which is usually revealed to the audience. In *The Absence of Malice*, we're not sure what Michael Gallagher (Paul Newman) is doing to save his good name, but by act three we know he's up to something that will significantly impact everyone involved in the accidental conspiracy. In action films the enemy's ultimate weakness is found and a final battle plan is put into action. In little films the hero finds a way to resolve the problem. In *Orange County* the lead character determines that if he can't get into Stanford, he must at least meet with the famous writer who teaches there because the writer is the reason he wanted to attend this particular school. When he comes out of that meeting, he has resolved his problem.

There are a couple of important things to remember with regards to the all-consuming climax. The protagonist must be on screen and involved in the action. We want to see the main character doing battle. It is recommended that the protagonist and the antagonist meet face-to-face. Nothing is quite as satisfying as the two opposing characters actually confronting each other, looking each other in the eye, and battling to the end, whether with weapons, fists, or words.

In our example, the young woman may reach the outskirts of Los Angeles. She stops on a rise and views the city below. Looking at her smoking, dinged-up car she gives it a pat, gets in, and sputters on to her goal, coaxing it each mile of the way. Finally she confronts her mother personally, or her film's director, or whoever is appropriate, depending on the plot you've hung on this premise. In *Beverly Hills Cop*, Axel comes face-to-face with the antagonist in the midst of a huge gun battle. The same is true for *Witness*, and even in *Payback* Mel Gibson's character faces off with the bad guys and the bad cops, although he only exchanges a look with the officers when they glance out the apartment window at him before the room they're in blows up. It works for all genres. In *Something's Gotta Give*, Diane Keaton's and Jack Nicholson's characters meet face-to-face in a Paris café, each with an escort, at the film's climax.

The thing to remember is that the audience shouldn't know the resolution before it is revealed in the climax. And after the climax? You are finished. The audience, now having been satisfied that the question that was raised has been answered, is no longer particularly interested. You've got to close it down.

This brief post-climax section of the screenplay is called the "denouement." You wrap up the loose ends and say good-bye to the hero. In Westerns, the hero rode into the sunset; in romantic comedies, a wedding or the promise of one is the conventional ending. In *The Graduate*, the subversive, countercultural point of view twists convention when the confused, clueless couple rides off in a bus.

SCENES

The building block of all films, the material that forms each act, is the scene. Scenes tell the story in small sections, a little like book chapters. The essential purpose of all scenes is to push the plot forward, and to reveal character. There are enrichments that can be added to scenes such as including elements that can illuminate your theme, but building the plot and developing characters are primary.

More specifically, in act one each scene helps set up and launch the story. The scenes introduce the characters and give us a very brief portrait of their personalities and their relationships; establish the setting, time period, and social strata; and dramatize the inciting incident and reveal the hero's decision or inevitable response to the situation the incident has place him in. So each of the scenes you write needs to serve one or more—we hope more—of these functions. Don't forget that the special responsibility in act one is to create an exciting, intriguing, curious, action-filled, or charming opening scene. It has to be something that makes the audience glad they came and keeps them in their seats.

The scenes in act two will focus on the complications you have arranged that will sweep the plot on its way, enable us to get to know the protagonist and the antagonist better, introduce subplots and new characters, and dramatize the theme of the work.

Action can lag in act two, and if writers aren't careful, their story will wander off course. You have to make certain that you keep the action going and the final climax of this act is always in sight.

Sometimes, if things are laid out well in the previous acts, act three almost writes itself. The primary goal of all the scenes in this act is to get the story to its apex of action and resolve it. We know the hero. There won't be any new subplots introduced. The tension in these scenes must be higher than at any time previously in the story; the stakes can go no higher; time has run out. If the pace was a trot in act two, here it is a gallop.

Scenes are microcosms of the full screenplay or the act. There is an arc to each scene. You set up the scene, and then build to the scene's climax. The young woman who took off across country can serve as an example. Perhaps she has run out of money. She's been driving all night and now she's hungry. There's not a bit of food in the car, just empty candy wrappers. She sees a diner and pulls in.

The scene in the diner raises the question: How will she get something to eat, or will she? The audience wants to watch because they want to see if she has the nerve to do something socially risky, and to see if she will succeed. The climax is the resolution of this question, whatever that may be. The answer should be held to the end of the scene, just as the screenplay as a whole holds the climax to the end. The diner scene zeros in on the girl's efforts and how the waiter or waitress responds to them. She can't simply come in, ask for food, and be given some. If you do it that way, there will be no tension, no buildup, essentially no scene.

If the waitress is kindhearted and charitable, there still needs to be tension. Maybe it develops between the waitress and the manager. Maybe the waitress looks angry or stern but underneath is a softie. Perhaps the young woman is so embarrassed that when she tries to make her case, she can't go on with it and the waitress takes pity but has to sneak her something from the kitchen. There are at least a dozen ways to handle this scene. The choice you make is determined by the plot you've outlined, by what you want to reveal of the hero's personality, by what you want to say about life, or because you want to expand on your theme or reinforce the mood you're trying to create. Whatever choices you make, it is important that the tension of this scene must build to the payoff. Once the question is answered, i.e., paid off, the scene is over. The way you *end* it is also dictated by your plot and character revelation goals. You should know before you write the scene how you want it to end.

Each scene must have a reason for being included in the screenplay. Before you begin a scene, ask yourself what purpose it serves. Once you know that, you will have a direction and a goal. If you don't know why you are including a particular story block, delete it. It will lie dead on the page and it will be obvious to all that the story stalls because of it.

Scenes, like building blocks, should line up seamlessly to create each act. Each act in turn combines with the others to create a screenplay that feels complete, whole, and satisfying, and whose under structure serves it well, but the outline of which is obscured by layers of story.

7

Putting Words Where They Belong: The Dialogue Challenge

You already know that when cinema first began, films were silent. There was no means of reproducing sound. Organ music was soon added to aid the audience and capture the moods and feelings portrayed on screen. Sometimes dialogue cards were inserted between scenes to enable the audience to follow parts of the story that simply weren't visual. The industry almost immediately began experimenting with methods of adding synchronous sound.

When a viable system for applying a soundtrack to the actual film was developed, as rough as it was, it ushered in a whole new era. Movies changed from all action and movement to "talking pictures." Actors had to huddle around a microphone hidden somewhere in the scene in the early "talkies," but it wasn't too long before boom microphones were developed and things got a little more natural. Established, reputable writers such as F. Scott Fitzgerald and Dorothy Parker were wooed to Hollywood to lend their writing talents to this new art, now dependent on words.

But even as Al Jolson spoke his famous line, "You ain't seen nothin' yet," many people were convinced that sound was a fad, another ploy by Hollywood to draw people into their gilded movie palaces. True cinema was silent; true cinema was telling stories with nothing other than moving pictures. But the audience also spoke. They flocked to the new movies with sound coming from the actors' own lips.

DIALOGUE LITE

Through the years, a blend of sound and action told each movie's story, although in the past couple of decades, the visual element has come again to dominate, especially in action films. It isn't any artistic retro movement. It's about lightweight cameras, computer-aided effects, and editing equipment that permits mobility. Once again, film is tapping a lot of resources to tell tales primarily with pictures. And, too, American films now have a worldwide audience with many pictures doing much better business overseas than at home. Playing to an international market challenges producers to convey their stories through universal emotions and actions, while using as little English dialogue as necessary.

A third force at play in the reduction of dialogue is the notion that younger audience members have grown up on so much media spouting so many short, fast messages that they simply won't focus on anything for very long; ergo, long passages of dialogue on screen slow the pace and is assumed to create boredom on the part of the viewer. Whether this is true or not remains to be seen.

As a screenwriter who wants to succeed, you need to keep the brevity of the dialogue in mind as you write. To help you create dialogue that will serve rather than sink your screenplay, let's review some basics.

WHY ARE THESE CHARACTERS TALKING?

One of the primary uses of dialogue is to help the plot move forward. If one character reveals important information to another, the audience has gained more information about the story.

Dialogue can indicate a character's current emotional temperature. Although it might be better to show this, if it's necessary to know more precisely what the character's feeling, sometimes a line of dialogue can define it more specifically than an expression or action. In *2 Days in the Valley*, a character grabs his abdomen and cries out in pain. We know he is in pain from the action, but dialogue quickly supplies the diagnosis: kidney stones.

Providing clarity for those elements that aren't visual is another important function of dialogue. A character might explain how a bomb operates so that the audience and the characters in the scene understand the urgency, extent, and implications of it exploding. The audience can see a timer, but if it's more complicated than that, a line of dialogue explaining how it works is appropriate. Remember the flux capacitor? It was important that its function was understood so that Marty McFly could get *"Back to the Future"* after his unintended trip to 1955.

There are also nonvisual elements of a character's personality that may need some amplification. The audience wants to see how the character behaves, but sometimes the character's back story can best be conveyed by dialogue, as can some characteristics. We might watch the character constantly putting gum in his mouth and assume he's trying to quit smoking, but we need dialogue for confirmation.

The back story of the plot or plot elements is often revealed by dialogue. It can be faster and easier to simply express in a bit of dialogue. For example, in a screenplay about an inner-city high school gone to seed and terrorized by student thugs, a character can look at an old photograph and explain that the high school had been the premier school in town and then switch to a visual of the current state of the school.

Dialogue is extremely important for establishing your characters' social skills, social standing, background, level of education, place of birth or residence, and often their profession or where they work. It can also reveal personality by the manner in which your characters speak. Do they speak slowly and precisely, or rapidly, or slur their words, or mumble? Is their vocabulary and word usage particular to a group? Remember Valley Girl–speak? Each of these approaches to speech says something about that particular character.

Dialogue can establish the tone, time, and type of film. We've all seen science-fiction films set in the future in which the speech is formalized, a stilted version of everyday speech. It's done to prevent it from sounding contemporary. Likewise, dialogue can immediately establish a period in history, almost as fast as the costumes and setting. Listen sometime to the dialogue in a tough crime drama, like, say, *Payback*, and hear how very differently these characters speak compared to those in a high school comedy.

It's difficult to know how people actually spoke before recordings were made, and even if you could duplicate it, no one could understand what your characters were saying. Speech constantly changes, as do the rules of grammar and usage. The best approach is to modify the dialogue so it gives the general impression that it is speech that might be heard in the era of your story. Researching books published during the time in which you have placed your screenplay will be very helpful. And you know you should avoid any contemporary slang or neologisms that have recently been added to the language. *Masterpiece Theatre* often features dramas that are masterful at catching the sense of earlier eras without actually attempting to replicate the speech of those times.

SHORT AND SWEET

Visual images always have more impact than speeches, so be ruthless with yourself. Don't indulge yourself by writing pretty dialogue. Use what you need and rely on the visuals. Many writers, especially new ones, don't trust visuals to communicate what they want to say, so they pile on the dialogue. They assume a double whammy should get the message across when in fact the audience is ahead of them, having "read" the screen more rapidly than the characters can speak. For an excellent example of how well action and facial expressions can substitute for dialogue, watch the Korean film, *3 Iron*. The main character in this film has no—repeat, no—dialogue throughout the entire film. And the romance that develops between him and a woman he has met also lacks dialogue until the very end, when a single line is uttered by the woman.

One way to approach dialogue is to ask yourself what dialogue is necessary, absolutely necessary. Maybe give yourself this quick writing exercise: Write an important scene in your screenplay without any dialogue. Write it again with only one line of dialogue. You can determine from this exercise whether or not dialogue is absolutely necessary or if the visuals are sufficient on their own.

Before you run screaming from your computer because you've been made to feel that using any dialogue in your screenplay is a sin, we need to back up a little. What you need to learn is how well you can tell a story without words. Film is a visual medium. On the other hand, dialogue is a necessity in many instances and an enhancement in many more. Shakespeare was all about words, as are all theatrical works. In many respects, movies are an outgrowth of theater and share many common elements with it. Some of our most memorable phrases came from a favorite movie and either made us laugh, helped us gain a new insight on life, perfectly summed up a particular emotion, or provided us with an articulate conversational comeback.

There are writers who are wonderful with dialogue, and their movies would be colorless without it. We go to those movies to see and *hear*. Wit is as important to screen stories as physical comedy, and repartee depends on spoken language. Robin Williams's humor uses both forms and each is important. The world would be a poorer place without Noel Coward, Neil Simon, Larry Gelbart, or the Coen brothers. So don't discount dialogue, just keep it in its place. Don't use it as a crutch, or a substitute for realistic or metaphorical visuals when they can do the job.

TWELVE TIPS FOR TALK

Writing dialogue is one of the hardest skills to master. So if your dialogue is less than dazzling in the first draft of your script, you are far from alone. Many analysts and producers are convinced that writing good dialogue is, above all else in screenwriting, dependent on natural talent or a natural ear for language.

When including dialogue in a scene, the following will give you some direction.

> *1.* Dialogue must sound natural, although it doesn't duplicate ordinary human speech. It is "movie-natural." The dialogue we all practice every day is often too slow moving, too mumbled, too tentative, and dull. In real human exchanges we hem and haw, repeat ourselves, and verbally stumble around. Movie dialogue is more interesting and movie characters, unlike us in real life, usually have a ready, witty comeback. Movie dialogue isn't real-life speech, but it must strive to sound real while fulfilling its function in the plot. On the other hand, trying too hard to sound natural can result in awkward, quasi-real

movie dialogue that's as false as it sounds. So, although film dialogue should fall within the general dimensions of natural human speech, it doesn't actually match it. Here again, movies push reality a bit.

2. In real life, people often don't speak in complete sentences or always think before they speak.

3. In real life, people are often elliptical—they understand each other with common code words and signs. The more intimate the relationship, the more that is communicated with less dialogue. An example: When long-married couples are ready to leave a party, they often have only to exchange a look and they have communicated their desire to say good night to the host. The characters in your screenplay can do the same.

4. When it comes to dialogue, the less you use, the more powerful each speech and each line will be. Make the speeches short and snappy. No one wants to listen to long, windy speeches. Besides, people rarely pontificate for minutes on end without interruption. Your characters shouldn't engage in any long-winded speeches either. There's another more practical, nonnarrative reason to avoid long, long dialogue: Many analysts and many more producers won't read it.

5. Don't let your characters imitate the movies. Many young writers who have little experience with life or with a variety of people from diverse social strata create dialogue that sounds like movie characters because it's based on movie characters.

6. In real life, people usually aren't direct. They rarely express exactly what they're thinking or feeling even when they assume they are. The stronger the feeling, the less likely it will be clearly articulated. When characters speak too directly about heartfelt emotions, it's called being "on the nose." It's too literal and it isn't natural, since in real life, most of our conversations are oblique. To understand how dialogue dances around issues without confronting them, watch the great American theatrical classic *Long Day's Journey Into Night* by Eugene O'Neill.

7. If you have important information that needs to be communicated in a scene, leave it for the end. Let the scene build to this payoff, tease

the audience a little with what the information may be, but use it as the punch line for the scene. It will make the audience curious and keep them involved.

8. Make sure each character has his or her own voice. One of the biggest complaints leveled at scripts is that all the characters in the screenplay sound alike and they all sound like the writer. Cover up the names of your characters in your script. If you can't tell which one is speaking, then you need to work on individualizing your characters' voices. Once you have your characters firmly in mind and see them as individuals, then appropriate dialogue should flow out of them sounding as natural to that character as it does with the people you meet every day.

9. The worst sin you can commit with dialogue is failing to make it interesting, witty, clever, smart, bright, and fresh. Give it some weight and a punch. One of the biggest complaints analysts have is dialogue that is full of clichés, flat, and leaden. Dialogue needs to surprise the viewers and keep them off guard by taking unexpected turns.

10. Sometimes the reason dialogue is too long is that characters are describing things we can see on the screen. Don't let your dialogue be redundant to action. In other words, if you can see it, you don't need to say it.

11. If you are positive that a particularly lengthy conversation is absolutely essential, break up the scene by letting the audience know with as few words as possible what the characters are *doing* while they're talking. Make sure they *are* doing something. Please, keep them away from tables and restaurants as much as you can. Movement of some kind is preferable. It is even better if what the characters do while they speak is worked into the plot and/or helps define the character.

12. One way to break up the long dialogue is to occasionally put in a camera direction. There's a very good chance it won't be used if it isn't crucial to an understanding of the scene, but it will break up the dialogue on the page, rendering it more readable. It is, of course, always preferable to include camera-angle directions only if they *are* essential.

LISTEN AND LEARN

As a writer, you should probably spend more time listening than talking. Note how people really speak. Fall in love with the sound of the language as produced by a diversity of people and the quality of their voices. One writer suggested going to a bar and listening to the conversations around you, but it works as well anywhere you go. Stop talking on your cell phone, stop plugging into your portable CD player or iPod, and listen. When people say something interesting, clever, funny, or striking, write it down. Eavesdrop on conversations.

One exercise that helps many writers is to hear your dialogue out loud. Listening to it will reveal whether or not it sounds like the natural speech of real people. Another suggestion is to get a group of actors to read your work. You will know immediately which lines don't work when spoken rather than written. It isn't an easy experience to endure, but it will be worth it.

TERMINOLOGY

There are two important terms that apply to narration and dialogue: One is "voiceover" and the other is "off screen." If you have a character who narrates or whose narration is not a part of the scene on screen, the lines are a voiceover, written (V.O.) in the script following the character's name. A character who is part of the scene but who narrates his internal thoughts, as Hugh Grant's character did in *About a Boy* and John Cusack did in *High Fidelity*, is doing voiceover. His dialogue is also labeled (V.O.).

A different term is used if you have a character who is a part of the scene, but is not on screen. For example, a girl's date has come to pick her up and as he waits in the living room, she finishes dressing in the bedroom. While she's dressing they converse. This is an off-screen character speaking, so it's written as (O.S.) and follows the character's name over the dialogue. Some people use (O.C.), for "off camera," to convey the same situation. "Off screen" is more common.

8

Elements of (Screenplay) Style

Getting the characters, the structure and plot, and the dialogue worked out until you're satisfied with them doesn't finish things. There are other potholes that can appear throughout your script that will give readers a rocky ride and diminish their opinion of your work.

This book is not meant to be a writing manual. There are no secrets you can learn that will *guarantee* writing success, but there are some common conventions and script elements that you should be aware of, and generally conform to, if you want your work to be taken seriously by the people in the film industry who will be reading it.

REFRESH YOUR ENGLISH GRAMMAR

Back in the fifteenth century, Erasmus said, "God does not much mind bad grammar, but He does not take any particular pleasure in it."

This attitude toward grammar—and punctuation and usage—holds pretty true for today's Hollywood. Because a script is the working plan upon which a movie—a visual presentation—is built, scripts generally aren't required to maintain the same literary standards that are required of material whose final form will be the print medium. Nevertheless, you should consider your screenplay as a semi-final form. Since it has to be read before it can be put on celluloid or disc, analysts need to drive through your prose with ease. When readers hit a trail of multiple misspellings, awkward usage, and errors in grammar, their "Sunday drive" through your story becomes a chore rather than a pleasure.

Oftentimes readers will not recommend a script if it is essentially illiterate. They also won't recommend the writer, who to the analyst seems genuinely oblivious to the common rules of grammar; they will sometimes recommend the story idea if it's a whopper, but it has to be the best thing since *Citizen Kane* (and you'd better have heard of that movie).

Every analyst reacts differently to writers who mangle, or even show disrespect for, the language. Some are more tolerant than others, but be assured, each has his or her particular bugaboos—errors they assume only an ignoramus would make. Probably the wisest approach is to strive to make your script flawless. It still won't be perfect; that there will be a missed typo or spelling error somewhere in its one-hundred-plus pages is practically guaranteed. So, although *you* may not be bothered that you're oblivious to the proper use of apostrophes or the then/than distinction, you don't know who may be reading your script. Whoever it is might just be a fanatic about the very rule you've disregarded.

If you're feeling a little unsure of yourself, begin your scriptwriting career by buying yourself an invaluable gift: a copy of Strunk and White's *The Elements of Style*. Read it through three times—it's only eighty-five pages long. Also, run grammar and spelling checks of your work, and don't ignore the problems they find.

You may be more devoted to the visual than the written, but don't sell those building plans short and hope that analysts will read your mind and understand what you mean to say, even though you haven't figured it out how to say it. If someone can't read your blueprint, your project will never get constructed. And don't hope to explain it all in a later pitch meeting. Putting descriptions on paper forces you to clarify what you're envisioning and will make your presentation much stronger. Relying on, "Ya know what I mean?" and, "Awesome explosions," and, "You know, that kind of stuff," won't get you any farther in a meeting than will an illiterate and unrealized description on the page.

CAMERA DESCRIPTIONS

Anyone who picks up your script should be able to read it and mentally watch it on screen. This means the reader should "see" the flow of the story without being bogged down by excessive material meant to be used by editors, cinematographers, and directors. Write a story script, not a shooting script. An assistant director or a unit production manager will work out the shooting specifics with the director and director of photography. For instance, an analyst may see the following:

> The camera tracks on the carpet, then angles up through the glass table and stops on Tiffany's ample cleavage, then tracks through the glass! It goes over her shoulder and does a 180-degree turn, and we see a knife sticking out of Tiffany's back through her designer dress. On a Steadicam, the camera tracks down the back of the couch, following the dripping blood. NEW ANGLE: From the kitchen to the living room, a shot of a fly on the kitchen ceiling. POV as the fly takes off and lands on the knife!

Excessive shot descriptions such as the one above aren't necessary, and they slow down the story's flow. More importantly, the director will consider the writer presumptuous for trying to usurp the creative challenges of his job. Contrast the above with this scene from *Chinatown*:

> On Gittes's desk, there are empty coffee cups, the summons and complaint— and the newspaper Gittes brought with him from the barbershop.

The cinematographer is free of unnecessary shooting instructions and will create camera angles appropriate to ensure the meaning of the shot is conveyed.

DON'T BE A TECHIE

There might be occasions when you need to describe technical information important to the plot. You may know everything possible about your arcane science, machine, or topic, but usually, the audience doesn't need to understand everything about it. Neither does the analyst.

Keep your prose nontechnical, brief, and essential to what will be seen and used on screen. For example, maybe you need to use a piece of obscure English law or a whatsit machine that performs some rare medical test; the law or the machine is important to your plot. If you feel you can't or shouldn't translate the law's meaning or the machine's function into everyday speech, are you sure you aren't showing off? Which is more important to you, to show off your knowledge, or to sell your script? Test out your rewrites on friends willing to indulge you. See if they understand what you're trying to explain.

WE'RE TALKING MOVIES, NOT BOOKS

To keep the flow going, limit your descriptions to what's *seeable* on screen. When introducing or developing characters, forget about describing what they are thinking. Unless you put this information in dialogue or use (V.O.), how will we know what the character is thinking or feeling when we see him on screen? We won't. Show us what action the character's thought or feeling engenders; then we'll know. It's a movie, after all, not a novel.

Always let your characters' actions and dialogue show us what kinds of people they are, what they feel and think about anything and everything that's relevant to the plot.

This rule holds true with the "mise en scène" (the entire contents of each shot). Don't write that the weather's always been rainy in whatever locale you've placed your story if the rain is never seen and doesn't work into the plot in some way or add a dimension to the characters' emotional states or to the story's theme. Why include it?

DESIGNER LABELS

Excessive descriptions of appearance and clothing also put the brakes on the forward movement of your story. It's easier on the writer and the reader if you state right away what status or politics a character's dress and accessories reflect. Don't become a Neiman Marcus catalog copywriter in the middle of the suspense tale you're hoping will grip the reader. Styles and designer names come and go, so getting too specific will date your script.

Excessive and precise descriptions (unless they figure into the plot or the character in a *crucial* way) tell us more about the writer's ideas of wealth and glamour than they do about the characters. Writing that a character "drives up in a late-model, expensive car" is plenty informative. The reader will get it. The exception to this rule is the handling of stereotypes. When and if you have stereotypical characters purposely included in your story, sometimes a particular type of car is a part of that stereotype. Then you will want to include the car's make. Say, for example, your script includes a Hell's Angel type. You would probably want to include that he drives a Harley-Davidson.

Don't be afraid to write descriptions. You don't want to be so uniformly literal and terse that there is no pleasure in reading the screenplay. The rule here is to keep your descriptions creative and brief.

The same holds true when introducing a new character. You want to avoid descriptions that are too lengthy and sound too much like a bureaucratic record. Instead of, "Jim, twenty-six, blond, measuring six feet, eight inches . . ." use a metaphor or more descriptive words. "Jim, who could be Apollo's stand-in . . ." or, "Jim, a Clairol blond who could play center for the Pistons . . ." There's just no getting around it: Colorful writing is easier to read, and you are, first and foremost, a writer.

WHY A MONTAGE?

Montages—those short, jump-cut, rapid shots, usually written without dialogue— are trickier than they first appear. They seem like an easy way to show a relationship developing or the preparatory steps for an upcoming action scene, but too often, they are a crutch for writers who want to cover some dull or difficult material quickly. The reader wants to get through montages because these moving snapshots usually contain little tension or conflict, and they rarely contain essential story material that will tie into the plot or a relationship later on.

One scene with carefully thought out action can serve just as well as a montage to reveal a growing relationship or a setup for subsequent action. In *Be Cool*, the writer could have used a montage showing Chili's (John Travolta) growing interest in Edie Athens (Uma Thurman) and in the music industry. Instead, the screenplay relies on the look on his face when he sees her; it reveals his newfound interest in her. His growing involvement in the recording business is revealed through his efforts on behalf of a new singer he's discovered and the comments he makes about his shift from film to music. It gives us all the information we need. Try and discover a better way to tell your story than lining up a series of one shots.

FLASHBACKS, FANTASIES, AND DREAMS

Flashbacks, like montages, are often a crutch for a writer hoping to fill in a character's background. The information imparted often isn't really necessary to the story's development.

When flashbacks are used, it's best if they're brief, and if you use several, they can form their own mini-subplot. If that subplot affects or works into the main plot, that's ideal. Before including flashbacks, ask yourself what purpose they will serve. Is there another way—preferably through action—the same information can be conveyed? Flashbacks can destroy a story's momentum, especially when they distract from the story's primary tale and nothing in them relates to it.

In some films the flashbacks *are* the plot, and they have a *significant* influence on the characters' present-day lives and circumstances by story's end. Essentially, the film's opening and ending in the present day simply bookend the story's plot. The plot tells the story of how these characters came to be who, what, and where they are at the story's closing scene.

Some films, like *Pleasantville*, use a kind of time travel—in this one, it's via the television—but essentially, it's a flashback. Other fantasy films, like *The Matrix* and *Groundhog Day*, manipulate time by stopping, replaying, and rewinding events. These, too, are another form of flashback, and/or flash-forward.

Blurring the lines between reality, dreams, visions, electronic re-creations, and paranormal experiences have taken over where the brain probes, sensory deprivation, and hypnosis of old left off. The purpose of many of these sequences is to confuse the audience into believing the dramatized events may or may not be real. *Secret Window* used this technique.

Before relying on these sequences, think through the decision carefully. Regardless of their ability to fool the audience or their shock value, these sequences, like flashbacks, can keep your story's forward thrust in neutral. And their shock value will work only once in a film; after that, the audience is on to you. Overuse can become a liability to your main story. If you decide to employ these techniques, make certain the analyst can follow your path, i.e., know in which state the characters reside at any given moment in the story. Don't let these excursions to Neverland or Never Was Land stop the forward flow of your story; tie them to the main plot in some way.

TELLING US ABOUT IT

Narration, so popular in the old film noirs, is always an iffy approach, though it's occasionally done, as it was in *About a Boy*. In some films, there's a little narration used at the beginning to help set up the story, but the focus quickly moves to the action. Like dream sequences and flashbacks, narration can become a crutch. If you're substituting words when you could use action, you're writing radio, not film. Whenever narration is included, it absolutely must serve a function in the story, and even then, any extended use of the narrator is hard to justify. Item to remember: There are people in the business who flat-out hate narration.

LAST WORDS

George Bernard Shaw once said, "In literature, the ambition of the novice is to acquire the literary language; the struggle of the adept is to get rid of it." In today's world, if literary pretense is diminishing—because no one's reading the classics anymore—it is being replaced by a hybrid, awkward approach to language. Apparently, too many writers are watching too much television—specifically talk shows, cop shows, reality shows, and advertising. They have allowed terms like "perp" and "proceeded" replace the terms "the guy/man/woman" and "walked/jogged/trod/ran/strode" that should have been used; and advertising descriptions, e.g., "a refreshing drink," have sometimes replaced descriptions based on real observation and appropriate to the context. It's no wonder that, as Katharine Hepburn said in *The Philadelphia Story*, "all that . . . corkscrew English" shows up. We're assaulted with it every day. If it isn't pouring in from television and advertising, it's coming from the bureaucrats or the commentators, scholars, and "experts" who constantly explain our own society to us in psychobabble or in the language of the business or legal fields. Think of yourself as Shaw's "adept" and clear all this clutter out of your writing.

NAILING THE PLOT TOGETHER

Below are some tips on how to keep your script cohesive, precise, *and* engaging to analysts and producers.

Length

Currently, the scenes in screenplays run about two to three pages. The old conventional eight- or ten-pager is probably too large of a narrative chunk to tackle all at once. If your scenes run five or six pages, maybe you're trying to do too many things simultaneously. This is easy to solve. Clearly identify the purposes of the scene and the scene's climax that you're writing to reach. Once you know what you're trying to achieve, break the long scene into two or three shorter ones, each of which serves fewer plot functions.

Keeping It Alive

If your script includes a big action scene, don't toss it away by writing something like, "Right here should be the biggest gang fight you ever saw," or, "At this point, all the planes attack." You most assuredly don't want to wrap up an action scene in a sentence like these if that scene is the story's climax. Writing an important action scene in this manner will diminish its impact, and it makes you sound as if you're uninformed or too lazy to think it through and figure out how to write it.

When guns are important to the scene, you should know one from another. You don't need to join the NRA, but you should be able to distinguish an AK-47 from a .38. It's even better if you know which guns have what reputations.

To choreograph a commando attack or similar scene, work out the logistics in your mind, or on paper, before you write it. Then write it and rewrite it, paring and refining it.

Following the actions of many characters, in different locations, in a variety of vehicles, toting different makes of guns, can drive a reader to distraction. If the reader can't get a picture of the battle and has to go back over the material to keep track of who is where and who's been killed or wounded, it's frustrating. You must describe the chaos you want to convey with clarity, coherence, and brevity.

If you have a complicated action scene to describe—say, a gang of burglars is breaking into a top-security government building—you need to describe how it's being done. Again, think it through. If the break-in isn't described in realistic terms, you'll lose the audience's goodwill and willingness to believe in the story. And if the description of the action scene runs on for several lines, break up the paragraph with either a simple double-space or a camera direction, such as, "ANOTHER ANGLE."

Wow Them

Since your script will be read before it's put on screen, dazzling the readers along the way will improve your chances of selling the material. For that reason, try to include at least one scene (the more the better) that will sweep the readers off their collective feet with its cleverness, uniqueness, and dialogue.

In the words of the late Gary DeVore, writer of such films as *Running Scared* and *Back Roads*, and former head of production for DeLaurentiis Entertainment Group, "Every script should have one unforgettable scene and at least one line of unforgettable dialogue." Think of the scenes you remember from movies. Think of all the quotable movie lines you've heard.

If you can manage Herculean creativity for at least one scene and produce a dazzler, it'll aid your script in many ways.

ABOUT LOVE AND SEX AND ROMANCE

Nearly every script written has a love story in it. Sometimes it's the central story, sometimes it exists for the convenience of the leading character, sometimes it involves a minor character and not the protagonist, and sometimes it's included so a sex scene can be a part of the story. They're a challenge to write well.

A convincing love story must speak to your audience with conviction. It helps if the writer has actually experienced romance. Experience beyond the high school crush kind of romance, or the short-term, noncommittal, experimental, college-kid kind. It is better if the writer has experienced the grown-up kind of love. The *As Good as It Gets* kind. The kind that reveals that the writer understands and appreciates, or at least tolerates, how the sexes work, individually and jointly. The esteemed screenwriters Garson Kanin and Ruth Gordon had a very long, successful love affair and wrote classic romantic comedies like *Adam's Rib* and *Pat and Mike*. They understood the territory.

Paint-by-Numbers Love Objects

The most disappointing element of a script is often the love story. There is such a sameness to so many of them; you would think the writers consulted the same muse. These scripts go something like this: In the opening pages of the story, the hero is confronted with the problem that fuels the plot. In the midst of this, he sees 1) the most beautiful woman in the world. She has 2) a perfect shape and 3) perfect clothes. She is usually self-confident and assured, able to take on any fight with anyone and win because she's so buff, and she regularly outsmarts just about everyone. When the hero fails, she's there to offer a solution, sometimes involving tag-team fistfights with the enemy. Conversely, if the hero wins the day, she's there, ready to congratulate him.

Omitting It

You can write great scripts without pasting on some unbelievably stilted romance if your personal experience doesn't quite give you the insight into how romantic relationships work. There are lots of good movies in which the love story was very sweet and adolescent. Remember *Star Wars*? And there are films that only hint at love, such as Bill Murray's *Lost in Translation*. Lots of terrific movies have no love story at all.

Cleaning It Up

Sex scenes offer another challenge. Obviously, they aren't the easiest things to write or to film. If you include a sex scene in your script, it's probably to show 1) a couple falling in love, 2) a couple profoundly in love, or 3) an erotic mood or coupling. Because it's too easy to get a response you hadn't intended, you have to proceed gingerly.

If readers laugh when their temperatures are supposed to be rising, or if they get uncomfortable when they're supposed to be cheering on the budding love affair you're writing about, you're in trouble. Keep your sex scenes conventional. Or, if the tone of your film demands being demure, cut to a new scene if the action gets too steamy. The sex you depict shouldn't be offensive. You're writing for a mass audience.

IS IT REAL?

Cinema is called the "realistic medium," but we know differently. We accept that movies take liberties with reality. Think of the last screen fistfight you saw. The hero, after taking a beating that would put any real person in traction for life, gets up, fights back, and eventually vanquishes his attacker. We know this isn't realistic, and many people decry this kind of fantasy for serving mankind badly. Similar, but louder, concerns are expressed about screen gun battles. This expansion of reality is one of those conventions that is so much a part of film, it's routinely included in movies and accepted as valid storytelling.

Since heroes are usually required to be somewhat larger than life, writers are permitted to color outside the lines of reality to tell their story. The degree to which a hero's abilities are enhanced depends on the script. In a live-action and computer-generated cartoon, such as *Sin City* or the *Mummy* films, the sky's not even the limit. But if your story is set in the more realistic confines of everyday life, as it was in the films *Crash* or *Vera Drake*, your hero's physical actions must be much truer to the capabilities of ordinary men.

A sense of appropriateness is the key here. If a story that is written fairly close to real life suddenly includes a scene that's straight out of a Schwarzenegger action film, it throws off the tone completely and becomes a jarring interruption.

Taking Liberties with Reality

It's acceptable to take liberties with the tools, techniques, and paraphernalia of various professions. For example, if, during your research, a technician tells you that certain kinds of data are unavailable on a computer screen, but in order for your story to advance in a visually interesting way, or because it seems the most efficient way to convey some vital information quickly, you want that information to appear on a monitor, then show it on the screen. You've expanded reality. You haven't created impossibility, you've just embroidered on accepted technology.

Physics

Don't forget the basic laws of physics. An otherwise well-written script included a scene in which two goons wanted to shut down the power to a building in a Western city. The script describes them as being in the desert. They cut through a power pole, wrap some rope around the wires, attach the rope to their bumper, and drive off, felling the pole and breaking the wires. This act was supposedly committed by henchmen for a group of shady businessmen. What's more, the gang in the building to which the power was cut immediately jumped in their cars and drove to the desert power lines to find the source of their trouble.

There are so many things wrong with this scene that it should be part of a Three Stooges movie. Here are some of the reasons why:

1. How did the guys in the building whose power was cut know exactly where to go to find the culprits?

2. How do the goons know which way the current is running?

3. Main lines in the desert generally feed maybe half a city or more.

4. These wires aren't the size of that extension cord you keep in the bottom drawer in the kitchen; their weight helps stabilize the poles.

5. It's a good bet that these idiots would get electrocuted.

If you flunked high school physics, you really ought to do a little basic research before you write about complicated topics and maneuvers. Once you know what's physically possible, you can then stretch the scene to movie proportions.

Sci-Fi Rights and Wrongs

Science fiction presents special problems. Too often, authors of scripts that tell an out-of-this-world tale haven't got their physics in order. This might seem too elementary to even warrant discussion, but in one unfortunately memorable script, outer-space aliens came to earth possessing superhuman powers. It soon became apparent that whatever narrative problems the writer came upon, he solved by having the aliens possess a power to solve them.

When you create a new world, you have to work out what physical laws your beings or your worlds are going to obey. Superman, Batman, Spider-man, the Mummies, and Beetlejuice all have consistent limitations and powers.

Shangri-Las

A variation of this principle needs to be honored when you create stories about earthbound colonies or new societies established away from ordinary society as we know it. In one script, a writer depicted the creation of a new society established on an island. He lost the reader when he included materials that would be impossible for the inhabitants to possess. It worked for *Gilligan's Island* because that was supposed to be silly, but if you have some notions about the ideal society and you write a script dramatizing its creation, you have to restrict yourself to what's available to your characters.

Getting Real

Failing to do simple research is a much more common problem in regular scripts than it is in science fiction or idealistic society stories. The writer resorts to stereotypes or blatantly misrepresents characters or places because he hasn't gotten away from his computer long enough to actually explore his topic.

One script told the story, supposedly based on an actual event, of a contemporary Southwestern Native American man accused of murder. The writer apparently had never been around contemporary Indians. He wrote that the tribe killed animals only when they needed food. As anyone who lives in the Southwest can tell you, contemporary American Indians get most of their food from supermarkets. A little later in the story, the heroine explains, "Indians only burn dead wood." Forgetting for the moment that green wood doesn't burn well no matter who lights the match, a little dab of research, just a little, and the writer would have learned how dated, mindlessly romantic, and flat-out wrong he was. In Arizona alone, one Native American tribe once owned a huge logging company. No, they didn't burn dead wood; they cut down trees and sold them for a profit—like regular businessmen.

The writer revealed such an ignorance of his topic that his story became an insult, not a glorification, of Southwestern Native Americans. And it must be remembered that many tribes today have built casinos on their reservations. That's a big, sophisticated, and definitely not a nature-based business that has brought wealth to many of them.

DON'T UNDERESTIMATE THEM

You may assume on occasion that your fellow man is pretty stupid and spend part of your time feeling superior to him, but even those who lack sheepskins and whose IQs are in single digits catch on pretty quickly to characters' emotions and the plot turns in a movie. You don't need to hit the audience over the head with your ideas, characters, or plot twists. The writer of one action film reassured the reader every few pages that the hero's mission was dangerous. Enough already! Just show us some action and the audience will connect the dots.

EXPOSING THE MECHANICS

When screenwriters need to inform the audience of particular pieces of information to enable them to follow the story line, it's called "exposition," or, less formally, "laying pipe." Most exposition is handled in dialogue and action. Sometimes, however, there is additional information that needs to be conveyed. It ranges from the simple definition of an obscure term to explaining how a machine or a character "works." If exposition is poorly handled, red flags pop up all over the page screaming "exposition" and the audience knows your characters aren't talking to each other, they're talking to the audience.

To set up the plot, the author may need to explain how a machine works. Stay away from characters giving long-winded explanations. If you do, the exposition flag will fly, and the analysts will have to guzzle lattes so they can stay awake in order to read your work. There are at least a couple of ways to avoid raising the flag. One way is to have the machine go on the blink. While the crew tries to fix it, the audience gets the explanation, i.e., exposition, they need.

Another approach is to have two characters argue about the usefulness, value, or ethical problems of a machine. Through their shouting, they explain just what it is that the contraption does. Keep the argument short.

Delineating the author's message is a more common exposition problem than either of the above. This thesis is usually the reason the author wrote the script. You know these scenes; they come about twenty-three minutes into every television sitcom. The characters realize Something Important About Life. The "author's message" flag waves like crazy. In a screenplay, you must be more subtle. Your message, the script's theme, must be woven throughout the action, and if you've told your story well, the audience will have gotten it by the denouement.

NOW IS ALREADY THEN

Attempting to write to a trend or in anticipation of one is a bad idea. With incredible luck (emphasis on *incredible*), the time it takes to get a film produced is about three years. So, if you've written a trendy piece, chances are the trend will be spent by the time your story reaches the big screen.

FOLLOW THE MONEY

Anticipating the budget necessary for your film is an exercise in futility. No one ever sold a script based solely on the cost to produce it. Concentrate on writing a good story; let the studio worry about the budget. The cost of a movie isn't your responsibility; marketing your gem is. If you've written a huge historic epic, don't submit it to a company that makes only forty-million-dollar movies. Write the story you want to tell without regard to budget. Then, when you're ready to sell it, find an appropriate company.

TITLES ARE IMPORTANT

Sometimes you change the title of your screenplay repeatedly; sometimes the title comes as pure inspiration. You might want to try out the name on a few friends before you chisel it in stone. Don't underestimate its importance—titles can become cultural catch phrases. We're still using "back to the future" in various contexts, and permutations of "sex, lies, and videotape" are still with us. Even "the Terminator" is still invoked, and not just in reference to Arnold Schwarzenegger.

Your script's title ought to be appropriate for the genre of film you're writing. By trying it out on your friends, you'll find out if it implies a tone for your movie that you didn't intend. For example, sometimes a script title can read like a comedy, but the story is anything but funny. Other titles sound downright tragic, but the story's as lightweight as a cream puff. Think for a minute of the difference between *Jaws* and *A Fish Called Wanda*. Even if you didn't see these films, you can figure out from the titles which one is the comedy. How about *The Money Tree, It Grows on Trees,*

Greed, or *Wall Street*? All these films are about money, but there isn't much doubt about which films are comedies and which aren't.

Many film titles tend to be short so that they quickly convey the movie's high concept: *Crash*, or *Sahara*. Sometimes titles are familiar phrases or clichés that have an ordinary meaning and also reflect the theme of the story or refer to an additional, sometimes a symbolic meaning: *Fever Pitch*, *Kicking & Screaming*, and *As Good as It Gets*. Of course, the real winner in the title sweepstakes is coming up with an original turn of phrase that will be quoted from the day the film's released.

THE HEART OF IT

"Write from the heart" is advice that is often given to new writers. What does that mean, exactly? The notion of writing from the heart is an erstwhile romantic sentiment and a warning to the novice. If you're a professional writer, accustomed to making a living by putting words on paper, your heart doesn't necessarily have to be present and accounted for every time you write.

There's a story told about Laurence Olivier, considered by some to be the greatest twentieth-century actor, when he was working on *Marathon Man* with Dustin Hoffman. Hoffman was completely involved in preparing for a scene, getting inside the character, tiring himself out so he would have an appropriately haggard look. Olivier, opposed to such elaborate tactics, walked by, saw him, and said: "Don't live it, just do it."

If you're a novice, however, writing about that which you care deeply is important. Otherwise, you won't have the will to finish it and undertake a campaign to sell it. Completing over a hundred pages of narrative is a challenge, especially for those with no practice at it. There is no guarantee that just because you are writing from the heart, the script will be good or will succeed, but you're more likely to fight for it if the material is meaningful to you.

Most important, if you write with passion, there's a real chance you can move the reader. If you can engage the analyst's mind *and emotions*, you've hooked 'em!

9

Stop Going to the Refrigerator and Start Writing

Perhaps you have told people, maybe your family included, that you are writing a screenplay, and they picture you sitting at a computer putting the words on paper like a typist.

People who don't write or have never been around working writers often think that once writers get an idea, they simply sit down and start typing it onto the page, stopping only to remember a particular word or hesitating after a sentence here and there to catch their breath and reread their work. The ideas in their heads come out as fully realized scenes, sentences, and dialogue—just as it was in your head.

More sophisticated people know that writers are required to think about what they're going to write, plan it, and make dozens of notes as ideas occur to them.

Writers like you know the reality. You are personally acquainted to the mean-spirited sprites that dance on your head and in front of your eyes when you sit down to write. Without warning they appear, paralyzing your typing fingers or creating havoc with the wiring in your imagination.

INTRODUCING YOUR PERSONAL SPRITES

Among the sprites that can arrive at your desk before you do are the spirits of the material itself. They roost on your monitor and bedevil you with self-doubt and story problems.

Act two of your screenplay is one of the places where these evil ectoplasmic-defying elves get pretty rowdy. You got act one. You got the story set up, introduced the hero, and created the event that forced your hero into taking action. If it went well, you wrote with some ease through the climax of this act.

Now you're facing down act two and the material is getting thinner than a runway model. What are you going to do until you get to the climax? Act two sinks many a writer, at least temporarily. It is the tough one to write. It is the act that develops character and plot, complicates everything, lets us in on some of the stuff under the surface, takes a peek here and there, and sets us up for act three and the big finale. Some scripts simply sputter out at about page forty-five or seventy or sixty-three when the story gauge hits empty.

If this is the sprite that's pinned you down, get to your outline immediately and rethink it. Movies don't go directly from opening to climax. So, if that's as far as you've gotten in developing your screenplay, then you still have a piece of work to do. Instead of sitting at the computer hoping the yellow brick road will magically materialize and lead you to Oz, you'd better get the mortar mixed so you can lay down your own throughway to act three.

Let's look at an example: A teenager's family moves to a new town and he has to enroll at a new high school. You know how to set all this up in act one, and maybe you've planned to have the climax of the first act be the boy's encounter with his antagonist. Act three will focus on the boy realizing that although he's tried and failed (act two), he now knows exactly what he has to do to achieve his goals that were set up in act one.

You've probably already decided where you want the boy to be by the final page. There are a dozen goals that he can pursue in this particular overworked concept. Is the boy looking for acceptance? Learning a new teen culture? Getting the girl he wants? Beating the school bully? Exposing the school punks as dope pushers? Making the team? Passing the math test and getting accepted at a good college?

If you can't get through act two with this material, you probably haven't developed it thoroughly. First, examine all the possible complications that could occur to the boy as he pursues his quest. Make a list of all the things that could or might happen. If, for example, the boy is trying to achieve acceptance at this new school, what might prevent that? What might aid that? The growing conflict in each act isn't a simple arc; positive and negative events happen that eventually push the characters to the climax. Where does the boy go for solace during his fight? Do you have a character who fulfills that need? How could the subplot be worked into the primary plot? What other problems does the boy have? Consider developing texturizing subplots that provide more complication and cultural variety to the main plot and/or add color and depth to the characters. For examples, watch *Crash* or *About a Boy*. In this story idea, there are lots of subplot possibilities. For example, what about the boy's relationship with his parents? What about their problems in this new town with new jobs? What does the boy do when he's not at school? What about the antagonist's activities? What about positive things the boy discovers as he marches toward his goal? Watch *Rebel Without a Cause*.

In the second act, let the audience get to know the protagonist a little better. Think of the last half-dozen films you've seen. It's generally in act two that the hero finally beds, or at least falls for, the love interest. And it is usually in this act that we get to know the personal side of the hero. We might see his other relationships, or we learn what he's really interested in pursuing after he dispatches the bad guys.

If act two is getting to you, sit down and rework, enlarge, and refine your outline. It will give you some guidance. Remember, though, don't pad it. The audience will know immediately that the plot's going nowhere and that those long-winded conversations you've included have no effect on the development of the plot. Keep anything extraneous, any irrelevant fluff, out of your work. Tight scripts are the ones analysts can't put down.

Maybe act two isn't your problem. Maybe in act one you've got a great opening scene and an unbeatable incident to launch the story. But you can put it all on paper in seven pages. Since act ones are usually somewhere between twenty-five and thirty pages, sometimes shorter—say eighteen or nineteen in action and comedy scripts—you've got a problem.

You should probably go back and write a good biography of your main characters and the antagonists. Review all the roles in this story of yours, make notes on all of them. Also, review what ability, quality, skill, or effort your protagonist will use to prevail in the climatic scene that resolves the story. That characteristic or that ability needs to be introduced early on. In many major films, that talent is introduced in the big opening scene of the movie. And don't slack on the setup. We need to see where this hero lives, how he lives, who he lives with, and the general outline of his life. Show us, particularly, his reaction to whatever happens to him that will bring him to a decision about the action he must take following the inciting incident.

In *War of the Worlds*, the audience is immediately introduced to Ray Ferrier (Tom Cruise) and very quickly learns something of his life, i.e., what he does for a living, where he lives, his marital status, and his relationship with his children. We also are shown that he is a man of conviction and some stubbornness—even if it only applies to refusing to work overtime so he can get home in time to meet his ex-wife and children. When his sense of resolve is called upon later in the film, we know he has this quality because it had been set up in those opening scenes.

Then, too, some writers agonize over act one because they've heard that producers and agents only read act one. Don't you believe it. They only read five to ten pages. But, now that you're even more concerned, focus on your story first. Goose up the first ten pages in the rewrites.

Maybe act three is your challenge. You just don't know how you want this story to end. You're having a lot of fun with these characters but you are not sure what will happen to them. You should know. Even if you change the content and the resolution of act three midway through your writing, you should know. If you don't, you probably haven't really thought about the direction of your story. You need to ask yourself again, "What problem does my hero have to solve, or what question does he need to answer, or what quest does he have to take, or what goal does he have to reach?" Once you remind yourself of your original design, it gives the entire script a direction. It doesn't matter whether or not the hero succeeds or fails; you know where he has to go. Remember *Orange County*? The hero wanted to get into Stanford. When it looked like all was lost to him, including his girlfriend, he met the professor-writer he idealized and realized he didn't need to go to Stanford to become the writer he was hoping to become. So, he failed to get into the college he wanted to attend, which was his original quest, but he discovered something much more important and the climax occurred on cue, just as it should have.

Office Space followed a similar pattern. The protagonist hates his job, and when he decides to let himself get fired, he gets promoted. The story follows a discernable dramatic arc. The hero decides to get the best of this heartless and joyless company. But after the series of events in act two, he discovers something important about himself; the spirit-deadening, poorly managed company gets what it deserves; and the hero finds a new job that he enjoys and sees the value of.

SPRITES TWO

It isn't just act two that can get you down and keep you from finishing. And it isn't always the material itself. Sometimes it's what happens when you write. The mischievous sprites invite their evil brothers over to plague you. They pop out and sit on your shoulder. They create such a racket that it's almost impossible to write. It's no wonder lots of writers take to drink.

You become unsure of everything you put on the page. You thought it was a great idea when it came to you. You loved it when you rolled it around in your head. You felt clever when you worked out the story. But now a creeping discontent, an unnamed worry is making its way across your neural synapses. Every word you write seems like the worst choice imaginable. The plot points you developed sit on the page as the least intriguing ideas you could have chosen, but nothing else comes to mind. You describe your characters and the words sneer at you. You wish you had paid more attention to that teacher who encouraged you to build your vocabulary. How could you fall so short of your own expectations?

You come to the conclusion that this story is the stupidest idea ever conceived. You visualize what will happen if you give it to any of your friends to read. They will meet up at the local coffee bar and spend the evening laughing their heads off at your ridiculous idea, your terrible writing, and your completely incomprehensible characters. You can't even let yourself imagine what an agent and his assistants will do.

You decide that the whole project, idea, and execution are the worst things ever brought forth from any currently functioning imagination. You wonder whether or not to shred the whole thing and look for work clerking at Wal-Mart or cleaning Holiday Inns.

Good, honest, physical labor has its blessings. One of them is the absence of self-doubt. It's not something you'll achieve as a writer; only the mediocre, and maybe the geniuses, are satisfied with what they write.

If you don't dispose of your script, you eventually begin to wonder if there's anything worth salvaging in it. You wish you could go back to the day you loved this idea. It's like falling in love. At the beginning it's new and heady. But now that you're getting to know your lover, serious doubts creep in, like a dense and choking fog.

Where do you go when these gremlins dance with wild abandon all around you? Take a pass on all the psychoanalysis handed down from the psychiatrists and psychologists in the first six decades of the twentieth century and all the pop psychobabble of the latter four. Sit down at your word processor. Let the little devils have their say for about ten or twenty minutes while you play hearts or solitaire or type repeatedly, "All work and no play make Jack a dull boy." Then tell them to go to hell; swallow hard and press on, promising yourself a complete and thorough rewrite of this drivel when you reach the final page. Paste Eleanor Roosevelt's words, "You must do the thing you think you cannot do," across the top of your monitor.

It's almost inevitable that your feelings will change again before you get to the end of your script. And there is a very good chance you'll feel better about the material later.

THE GREMLIN IS HOLDING YOUR ENDING FOR RANSOM

Have you met people who have never finished their doctoral dissertation? Or people who dropped out of high school just weeks before graduation? Or students who drop out of med school before they finish?

There is something about finishing. We all live on dreams. But once you finish a script, polish it, and dress it up for public presentation, the dream is laid to rest, replaced with sobering reality. Not only have you committed your imaginings to paper, with all the pain and pleasure that entailed, but now the story is no longer your private domain. It hardly belongs to you at all. You will get unwanted and unsought comments. People you try to sell it to will want to change it—a little or a lot. Your secret pleasure is gone and it can never belong exclusively to you again. Lots of writers just don't finish. They get into it maybe sixty or eighty pages and simply can't get themselves to continue, despite having act two worked out.

One way to handle this impasse is to put the thing away for awhile. Later, after you've emotionally separated from it, you can go back and take a fresh look at it. If you still like it enough to devote some more time to it, you will probably be able to finish it with clear-eyed dispassion. Conversely, you might pick it up at a later time and realize it isn't worth finishing. This script was a learning exercise. It served its purpose in your development as a writer. There's no need to finish it. Put it back in the bottom drawer. When you become rich and successful and studios are clamoring for more material from you, you can pull that one out, give it an ending, and go on with your next project.

ANOREXIC LITTLE DEVILS

A fourth kind of devil that occasionally haunts writers is in many ways the most fearsome. Occasionally you get deep into your material and you find it's running thin. You've reworked the outline and you've added material, yet it seems to be evaporating faster than a desert mirage.

It's not unusual for a college freshman to plan to discuss the decline and fall of the Roman Empire in an eight-page paper; writers sometimes try the opposite approach. They think their sensible little story will consume 120 pages. You've probably seen movies based on video games or television series, which are criticized for being short on plot. Some writers of thirty-minute stories can't, according to the critics, conceive a story that has enough plot to last 105 to 120 minutes. Sometimes plot-bare movies are referred to as one-joke stories. Remember the movie *Blind Date*? It had one joke, and it was one with whiskers on it. So there will be times when, despite writing careful outlines and taking mental vacations, nothing you do makes your idea work as a full-length feature film, or an hour-long television series episode. You've run it out. There's not much you can do but set it aside. Sooner or later, at the most unexpected moment, you'll be shaken by an epiphany and you will know instantly how to rework the story. Then again, unless you want to try a script consultant or get some fellow writers whom you respect to help you, maybe this project will just have to collect dust until the pages crackle and fall away.

Not to worry. You'll fall in love with another idea very soon and will be off on a new adventure.

Part 111
LOOKING LIKE
A PRO

10

Keeping Up Appearances

When analysts pick scripts or are handed a stack of them, they look for promising reads. That first look and touch makes an impression.

Paper copies of scripts get an immediate review when analysts look at the cover, bindings, and title page. They flip through the script and check the length. When they see things that make them swoon, like excessively long scripts, neon-orange covers, and long, long passages of description, they put that script back in the stack and look for another. Scripts are also often provided as electronic files on CDs or via e-mail. They too are given the fast once-over, so the rules apply to them.

Because you want to pass this first informal inspection, your screenplays must look like the most professional scripts that come across an analyst's desk or desktop. It should not call too much attention to itself. You want your story, characters, and brilliant dialogue to do that.

Right now, put your script or scripts on your desk while you read this chapter, or open it up on your computer. Every time your script doesn't follow the current conventions, make the necessary change. Save your radical thinking, your march to a different drummer, for the *content* of your work. Don't squander it on the simple appearance of the screenplay.

WELL WRAPPED

Brads are the only way to secure the pages of a script. Also known as brass fasteners, you can purchase them at most stationery stores. Brads win the popularity contest in script binding because they can be easily removed and the script can be taken apart, copied, and then rebound. If a reader likes your screenplay, copies are made so more than one story executive can read it. Even if only one executive reads the script, a copy is often made. Using binders other than brads makes it impossible to put the script back together after copying.

An additional minor point or two needs to be made about brads. Although scripts are printed on three-hole paper, only two brads are used—one at the top and one at the bottom.

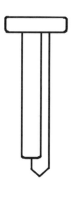

Figure 1

This seems to be done more from custom than for any practical purpose. It's not a big deal if you use three. Make certain that you use the proper-sized brass brads. For a standard screenplay, the one-and-a-half-inch length is a good size. (Figure 1) Make sure the brads are all brass. The others are too lightweight to hold the pages together. If the brads used are too short, the screenplay pages will pull apart before the analyst reaches the bottom of page ten. That will surely divert attention away from your story, and that is not good.

PACKAGE IT PERFECTLY

Remembering that binders should serve their purpose without screaming for attention, you'll want a little quiet from a cover. You want a little ordinary. And you want to remember that expensively bound scripts don't earn extra credit. The same applies to electronic files. The opening page should be free of vivid graphics and bright colors.

Paper scripts that are presented to production companies usually are bound in one of three kinds of covers:

The Cadillac of bindings, from an analyst's point of view, is made of two separate sheets of card stock—a little lighter weight than a file folder. They're neutral-colored, with an extended fold inward that protects the brads. The bendable cover eases transporting and holding the script as it is read. (Figure 2)

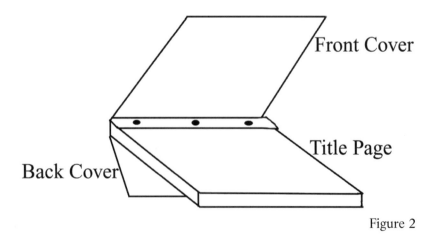

Front Cover

Title Page

Back Cover

Figure 2

A second type of cover, the second-most commonly seen on scripts, is the same-weight card stock as the first choice without the fold-in extension that covers the brads. This cover allows for ease in handling, but the reader will occasionally curse the brads when they get caught on something. (Figure 3)

Front Cover

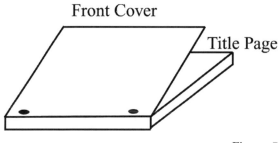

Figure 3

A third choice is to dispense with the cover completely. This is practically an essential for shorter scripts, such as those written for half-hour or hour-long television shows. The card stock, though bendable, becomes a bit of a burden when it's covering only fifty to sixty pages.

Script covers are recommended because they effectively protect the script. Without a cover, the front and back pages, maybe more, may get torn off as the script is handed from one person to another at a studio or production company. This isn't much of a problem with a short script, but it certainly happens to feature-length pieces.

Scripts are identified on the side closest to the brads, and then are usually piled on top of each other on shelves or lined up on shelves like books. If the title is visible, the script can be located quite easily. Specifically, the title is printed in block letters with a felt pen. If you submit a script in which the pages are encased in a cover, such as a folder, rather than bound between two separate pieces of card stock, it's impossible to label it in this manner. The script then becomes a small burden. Better if it isn't.

Create a cover for your CD, even if it's just simple paper, and print the title on the CD itself. It will help prevent it from being lost. At the very least, print the title on the CD. When e-mailing a script, send it as an attached file.

The cardinal rule is that the script's binding should never interfere with the presentation of the story. Therefore, covers are usually white, black, or anything bland.

If you think it would be appropriate or clever to cover your script in a color that reflects the story's theme or message, or in a binder with a picture on it, reconsider. It will not have the desired effect.

Think of it this way. Covers need to be analyst-friendly. Analysts have to hold the script as they read it and flip through it repeatedly when they write their coverage. If the brads are secure and covered, the script probably won't fall apart while it's being handled, nor will the brads scrape across the reader's desk and get caught on all manner of things. Also, if the cover is a neutral color, it won't distract the analysts' attention while they read your story, and if the cover bends easily while lending a little body to the script, so much the better.

SLIM AND FAST

Once the script is in the analyst's hands, the first thing he or she notices is the script's heft. If it's fat, the reader takes a deep breath and sighs—it will take forever to read the thing. The analyst wants to know the page count—this is especially true if the reader is a freelancer. Getting paid by the script means that analysts want to read as many as possible in as short a time as possible. Overweight scripts cause problems at all levels of development. Although movies at the local theaters run from about 90 to 140 minutes, writers without established reputations or previously produced works should stick to the accepted length.

Convention dictates that scripts run between 100 and 130 pages using Courier font in 12 point, not Times Roman. It is an important distinction to remember because the screen time is determined by the length of the script. One page of script in Courier 12 point is roughly one minute of screen time. Be on the safe side; limit the length of your script so it will fall around 120 pages or a little less. If your screenplay runs over 130 pages, you would be wise to cut it. You can cut it. You just think you can't. Read it again. You'll find an unnecessary scene, a description, or dialogue that runs too long. Trim it.

Conversely, anorexic scripts are also suspect. If your work's too thin because it runs less than 100 pages, read it through again. Are your scenes too elliptical? Will readers glean all the information they need from those scenes? Have you set each scene sufficiently? Does your story miss necessary beats? Check out your script, and see where a little more story needs to be told.

THE TITLE PAGE

After the analyst has given your script the once-over and made some initial judgments, the next set of impressions begins. Upon opening the cover, the first thing that comes into the reader's view is the title page—or it should be.

This sheet contains very little information and lots of white space. The name of your story should appear, centered and in capital letters, about twenty to twenty-five lines from the top of the page. Sometimes the title is in boldface. It doesn't matter. Some manuals will tell you to underline the title. Underscoring is standard format for television scripts, but feature film screenplays come both with and without their titles underlined.

Television scripts follow the title format above for the name of the program or series. Four to six spaces below this, the episode or segment title is capitalized, centered, and put in quotation marks. It generally isn't underlined. For example, if you've written a script for *Arrested Development*, the title would read: ARRESTED DEVELOPMENT. The segment or episode title appears thus: "THE MAN WHO WASN'T."

Credits

Four or five spaces below the title, also centered, in upper- and lowercase, the author writes one of four things: "By," "Written by," "An original screenplay by," or "Screenplay by." Most scripts use the simple "By," but it doesn't matter as long as what you write conveys the necessary information without getting in the way.

Two to four lines below the credit line, center and type your name in appropriate upper- and lowercase letters.

Contact Info

In the lower left or lower right corners of the page, at about line fifty-five, type your name, address (street, city, state, and zip), phone number, and e-mail address. If you have an agent, the agent will put his or her name, address, and contact number instead of yours or in addition to yours in the other corner. Putting your name, address, and phone number on the script is very important if you are not represented by an agent. The production company has to know where they can contact you.

That's it. That's all you need on the title page . . . Okay, there are a couple of exceptions.

Right to Write

If you've taken your story from another source, such as a novel, magazine article, or short story—that is, you own the rights or have contracted for the rights to the material—beneath your byline, you can include: "Based on the (short story) (novel) (magazine article)," and then name the literary source. You can also include the author's name in the citation.

If you've gotten your story from people you know or met or arranged to meet because their real-life experience is fascinating to you and you want to put it on paper, make certain you secure the rights to their story. You may not need to pay them a fee unless the story gets produced, but you should make arrangements to acquire the sole rights to develop a screenplay based on their experience.

And Be Sure NOT to Include . . .

There is information that many new writers seem compelled to include that shouldn't appear on the title page.

Don't include the date on the title page. If the date on the script is over a few months old, the reader will figure it has made the rounds and everyone has passed on it. Of course, it probably has made the rounds—almost every script does, even those from very well-established writers. But don't broadcast this information. If everyone has failed to see the gold vein that is your work, it's better to let each production company or analyst assume they are the first into the mine. Later on, if the film's a success, then everyone involved will be delighted to tell the story of how all the previous miners missed the mother lode. In short, you don't want your work to have a shopworn feel about it. Aside from feeling that the script has been turned down by everyone, a date that's long past makes analysts and story editors wonder if you've written anything lately. Do you only have that one work? And if you have a dozen, why didn't you submit your latest project? And finally, if you send out a script that has an old date on it, readers will wonder if the story is behind the times and less than fresh.

Telling story editors and analysts which draft of your screenplay you are sending them is also unnecessary and suggests that the writer lacks an understanding of the term "draft." No matter how many times you rewrite your script before you slip it into an envelope and head to the post office, it is the first draft. It will remain the first draft until you've made a deal and they ask you to rewrite it. Your rewrite, under contract, becomes the second draft and so on.

Including a draft number on the title page creates another minor problem for your work. When story editors or analysts see a draft number, they wonder if there is a newer draft you haven't sent them. And they question why you're telling them you rewrote the script so many times. It really goes back to the old saw that says pros make their jobs look easy. No one wants to know that Paul Haggis sweated over a weary computer keyboard to create *Crash* or that Nora Jones practices her scales for several dreary hours every day. We want to believe professionals do their jobs effortlessly. In the same way, although intellectually analysts know that writers worry over their scripts at least three or four times before they are presentable, no one wants to know that it took all that much trouble. Everyone wants to be told a good story and feel as if the teller is making it up on the spot. Remember, too, if you had a production deal and rewrote the script but the deal fell apart, start fresh. Take off the draft number. That the deal fell apart with another company is information the current analyst or producer doesn't need.

One final caution about title pages. Skip the WGAe or WGAw (Writers Guild of America East or Writers Guild of America West) registration number. It's irrelevant. The registration notice indicates that the script is the work of a neophyte, and a suspicious one at that. If you think that by including the registration number the bigwigs will be impressed that you actually know about the Writers Guild registration service and hence a little of how Hollywood works, you're wrong. Professional writers in Hollywood don't put that notation on their scripts. Every professional knows about the Guild.

Many top writers forego registering their scripts because they have an entertainment attorney to represent them in any dispute with a buyer. In other cases, the writer's agent is well known and sends the writer's scripts to various studios. Everyone around town knows who wrote the screenplay. If such high-profile writers registered their work, they don't make the notation on the material. It is a good idea for you to register your work, but don't include the information on the title page. Contrary to tales of wicked, wicked Hollywood, probably no one will want to steal your screenplay. Analysts and story executives read so many scripts that you should count yourself lucky if any can even remember yours. Besides, Hollywood is always looking for good writers. If your screenplay dramatizes the best idea to come down the Santa Monica Freeway in a long time and is beautifully realized on the page, the studio will want to be the first one to *discover* you. Instead of ripping off your stuff, they'll probably get you on the phone, pronto.

WHAT YOU DON'T NEED

Once the title page has been turned, the analyst wants to dive into the story. Ergo, page one of the script should follow the title page. Some writers seem to feel that if they provide lots of supporting information on the material, the studio will be duly impressed. This information often is slipped in right after the title page, or tucked into the script's final pages, or clipped to the script, or jammed in as an afterthought between the cover and the title page. Some writers send along enough information to fill a report folder. All of the information is superfluous and hardly ever read. The writers who want to succeed will avoid including the following material with a screenplay when they slip their script to a producer.

Cast of Characters

There is no need to include a cast of characters; it isn't a convention of screenplays. Adding a cast list signals to the readers that you think they are too dumb to follow your characters through the story and remember who they are. Did Tolstoy include a cast of characters in *War and Peace*? No. Did *The Aviator* flash pictures for us about who was who before the action got underway? No.

If you've introduced so many characters in your 110-page script that you're convinced the reader will be unable to remember them, then you've probably included too many. Remember, movies resemble short stories more than they resemble novels. They can't handle a multitude of complicated subplots, a vast number of characters, and the growth and change of a half-dozen protagonists. There simply isn't time. Miniseries, which no one in the United States seems to be making anymore, can do it. Feature films like *Gladiator* come the closest to succeeding at the chore, but even in epic, lengthy stories, we don't get to know all the various characters very well.

Casting Suggestions

Many writers pen their screenplays with a particular actor in mind to portray the protagonist. Please don't tell the studio who that actor is. Maybe, just maybe, you can comment in your cover letter that your main character is the type of guy that Brad Pitt or Tom Hanks could play, but go no further. Don't suggest who *should* play the role.

Studio chiefs and story executives have contacts with directors and actors and like to put together their own projects, unless, of course, an agent brings in a package, which also happens regularly. It may be that no one at that company has a relationship with the actor you have in mind. The director that's been chosen to head up the production may hate the actor you want, having worked with him previously. Even where there are no previous relationships, when a project is put on the production schedule and the studio gets serious about making it, the head of production probably will have an assistant create a list of actors who might be appropriate for the role if casting hasn't already been arranged. It's a list that can range from ten to seventy-five names.

Early in preproduction, a casting director is hired. He or she may or may not have a voice in casting the star roles. Casting directors bring their knowledge of what actors might be good and who might be available to fill all the remaining roles. They do the initial screening. When they line up some good candidates, the casting director and the film's director (and whoever else has a say in that particular production) audition the actors.

Executive decisions probably won't be influenced by your insistence that George Clooney play the lead in your project. What you might not realize is that stars such as Pitt and Clooney may not be available for a film role until 2088 because they are committed to other films, may have vowed never to work for the company or executive who bought your script, may have no desire to play roles like the one you've written, may have decided to take a couple years off, or any of a multitude of other reasons.

If the studio is interested enough in your script to make you an offer, you can *possibly* mention your casting suggestions in one of the meetings you have with the honchos. Until then, concentrate on telling a good story, and skip the suggestions.

Quotations

Some writers save the page following the title for a quotation, a pithy statement, a word of wisdom. The material presumably has something to do with the script's theme. Quotations in this context are a writer's conceit. They have nothing to do with anything. A script isn't a novel; its final form isn't printed material. No one but the analyst and, if the analyst likes it, a couple of story executives will ever see the quotation. So why bother? It won't be put on the screen before the story begins. If you want this wonderful piece of quoted wisdom to illuminate your theme, then put it in the mouth of one of your characters and place that in an arresting scene so viewers will pay attention to it. That's the best you can do. But putting it on a page by itself, letting it hang there in a no man's land between the title page and the story, the quotation becomes an affectation. It also signals to the analyst that the piece he or she is about to read may very well be so terribly, terribly literary and possibly pretentious that a solid, visually based, dramatized story which may deeply affect viewers will be sacrificed on the pyre of Saying Something Important.

As something of a last-ditch effort, you can try putting your quotation immediately following FADE IN. It might work, but probably it won't.

Synopsis

Why include a summary? Don't you want people to read the entire work? If you include a synopsis, there is a very good chance they won't. (Unless, of course, they are the analyst, who may be the only one to read this piece cover to cover.) There's a base canard heard throughout Hollywood that studio executives don't read scripts and agents can't read. If you give these guys a synopsis, well, draw your own conclusions.

Unless you're a first-class copywriter making your living creating unforgettable jingles, advertising catchphrases, or simple copy meant to sell a product, it could be that your synopsis will fail to encapsulate your stirring story. In fact, in the short form, your story may sound trite, or boring, or banal, or hackneyed. If you send it along, the story editor may immediately surmise that your script isn't the kind of material his or her company is looking for and return it to you unread.

Perhaps your story is just a little slip of a thing, but the characters, the location, and the theme are real knockouts. If you summarize the plot, the gem you've written won't be well represented at all. Don't give the studio any ammunition to shoot down your script before they've had a chance to read it through.

Scene Breakdown

Not many feature-film scripts received by production companies include a scene breakdown. However, some television spec scripts, especially scripts that are samples for a proposed television series, come equipped with a listing of the scenes. If a script arrives that includes a scene breakdown, it has usually been sent by a small production company looking for financing. The small company wants to show the larger one that preproduction preliminaries have been completed. None of this means anything to the story editor or the analysts. They will judge the script's story. It doesn't matter if preproduction work is already underway.

Scene breakdowns for television shows are done as one of the production steps after the script is bought and put into production. They aren't done by the nonstaff writer. Breakdowns for feature films are done early in the production process by the unit production manager, the line producer, or the first assistant director. They are part of the shooting schedule process; they are never done by the writer.

Screen Titles

Telling the reader, and ultimately the viewer, where and when the action's taking place through the use of on-screen titles is usually unnecessary.

The setting and costumes should tell the audience when the story's taking place. Occasionally, if the story hinges on something happening within a given space of time—say, a bomb must be found before it explodes—then using screen titles to indicate how much time remains may be useful. In most cases, it's not necessary. Did *The Aviator* include a title to tell us we were in Hollywood during the heyday of the 1940s and 1950s? No, we didn't need it. Usually the audience will learn from the dialogue and description what is necessary to know about the dramatic time period. *Pleasantville* is another prominent example. We immediately knew we were in pre–color TV days because the filmmakers used black-and-white film and the appropriate clothing and interior décor.

There are occasions when titling the location of a scene on screen is appropriate. If your screenplay revolves around a particular historic event, you might include time and place specifics in a title at the bottom of the screen. Say your story starts the night before the Columbine tragedy. A young man proposes to his girlfriend and she agrees. But she is so shaken by the morning's event that she changes her mind and dedicates her life to helping troubled children. In this case, it could be important that we know the specific date and time. War stories that focus on a particularly historic battle often include such titles.

Normally, the establishing shot should tell the audience where the story is taking place and the general time period. Establishing this information can also be accomplished through dialogue and other visual cues, so use superimposed information sparingly.

Pictures and Sketches

On rare occasions, usually with horror or anime scripts, a project comes into a studio that is accompanied by pictures or sketches. One of the joys of reading is using our imaginations. If you have creatures, machines, or chaos that you can't describe in the body of the work, then you may be in trouble. Including drawings, even as a single introductory page at the opening of a screenplay, isn't a good idea. They're like schoolboy doodles. Besides, it will be insulting to the film's director, the art director, and the director of special effects. Creating the look of the film's particular sets or characters is their art and craft.

A WORD ABOUT FORMAT

After the first brief review of the script, analysts come to page one and settle in for what they hope will be a great read. Don't let your work fail at this juncture. If the screenplay isn't in the proper format, you are pretty much sunk. This is the worst sign of an amateur. You have to prepare your work in a form an agent or producer expects to see. One of the conventions of screenwriting is following the established and accepted format. Your script should reflect this look. You want it to look like you're an experienced writer, right?

There are now many good script formatting programs, such as Final Draft, that enable you to give your script the accepted, professional look. They are very easy to learn. But if you're not ready to invest in one of these computer aides, formatting specifics will be discussed in the next chapter.

STUFF TO KNOW ABOUT PRESENTATION

There are just a few other items to deal with before you submit your screenplay. You don't want analysts stumbling over roadblocks you've neglected to remove, because as soon as they do, the analysts are pulled out of the story. You want to prevent that at all costs. Keeping the following in mind will help:

Make It Neat

When a production company or an agency makes copies of a script, the employee manning the machine cares less about your material than he cares about reading his statistics textbook. He will whisk the script through the machine, put brads in it, and deliver it to the appropriate person. If a page or two is missing or crooked, he probably won't notice. None of this is in your control. It's just a minor glitch you have to accept. However, you should never let your script get *to* a production company's office in this condition. When that opus of yours hits the story person's desk, it should be as pristine as possible.

Clean and Straight

Each page of your script should be as white as it was when you pulled the paper out of the box. No fingerprints, no smudge marks, no jelly smears or cigarette ashes. Remember, if it's dirty, it will not only make a bad impression, it will be reproduced that way over and over and over. When you make copies of your script, check each page to make sure the copy machine hasn't spit out pages with the copy on an angle.

While you are checking pages for any that may have gone astray in the machine, also make sure that the printing is dark enough to be read easily. If there are pages printed in a noticeably lighter or darker tone, you ought to go back to your original and reprint it until all the pages match. Scripts whose printing varies from page to page are irritating and, again, will pull the reader away from the content and into the form.

Count It Out

While you're going over that script page by page and giving it the final once-over, also check the page count. Sometimes copy machines skip a page or two. No one notices until the reader realizes that the story doesn't follow from one page to the next. If the missing page includes crucial action or some information that's important to the plot development, the loss is critical. Even if no essential plot information is omitted, the reader will view a missing page as casualness on the part of the writer.

White Space

After you have finished checking these minutiae, when you're beginning to wonder if writing's about creativity or about clerical chores, flip through the script one more time. There should be lots of white space. The script pages shouldn't look crowded or dense. There is an apocryphal story that circulates around Hollywood that says that one well-known executive reads only dialogue. The story may not be true, but it's certain that many readers and executives skim as much material as they can. If most of your story is told in lengthy description, very little of it may be read. It's a good idea to maintain a positive ratio of white space to printed matter.

Numbering Scenes

There is a standard argument that arises whenever struggling writers convene. Some will insist scenes should be numbered. Others are equally convinced that scenes need no numbering. Additionally, there's disagreement about whether the scene numbers should be noted at both the right and left margins. These disputes can be easily resolved: Scene numbers are unnecessary.

Feature-film scripts are written in master-scene style. The author begins each scene with the appropriate notation of the interior/exterior, place, and time of day. The scene is described, and the dialogue and action follow. These master scenes aren't numbered at all.

Television sitcom scripts note each act and scene with a number or a letter. On the other hand, feature-film scenes aren't numbered until they are put into production.

To Be Continued

The use of the word "continued" at the bottom and top of every page isn't necessary. Again, this notation is added when the film's put into production, in order to aid camera direction. That is, it lets the director of photography and the camera operator know whether to keep the camera rolling or maintain the same setup even though the end of a page of script has been reached. If your formatting program includes this notation, you can override the default setting.

Asides

Some screenwriters regard their writing task as a casual exercise that must be gotten through in order for a fabulous screen story to be told. They let themselves get chummy with the reader by making little asides to them. For example, one writer offered the following:

> The car's gearshift suddenly slips into neutral, and it begins a slow descent down the hill. We knew this was coming, didn't we?

When an actor talks to the audience directly, it's called an "aside." He has suddenly stepped out of the world on stage, a world the audience is looking at through the "fourth wall," and reminded the theatergoers that they are watching a play. A screenwriter does much the same thing when, in the midst of creating a story, he or she suddenly comments directly to the reader. This particular technique isn't endearing or particularly professional.

Once you whip all the preceding items into shape, you will have removed many irritating roadblocks.

11

Getting Square with the Page

A screenplay is its own unique medium. It's not put on the page in the same manner as poems, novels, or plays. In part, screenplay format is as it is because film is a collaborative art, and the instructions and information must be quickly and easily grasped by producers, directors of photography, sound men, art directors, actors, and many others.

Because there is no editor between you and the "public" for your screenplay, it is the screenwriter's responsibility to follow prescribed formatting conventions so the work is presentable. Possible buyers will discard the work if it is not in proper format and assume the writer is an amateur.

What is screenplay or teleplay formatting? The no-frills answer is this: It is the manner in which material is placed on the page.

It *isn't* about character development, the story arc, or how to write action scenes. It doesn't have anything to do with the heart of your idea or the telling of your story.

It *is* about such mechanical things as: What do you double-space, what do you single-space, and what do you capitalize in a screenplay?

DEFINITIONS

Before detailing how a screenplay should look on the page, a few definitions of less obvious terms may help.

1. **Beat:** Various meanings. When used in formatting, it means a hesitation in dialogue or action. Within dialogue, it's usually written as (BEAT).

2. **Camera Suggestions:** This is information the writer can include in a script in order to indicate the focus of a particular shot (close-up, establishing shot, reverse angle, etc.). Don't include too many of these.

3. **Con't or CON'T:** Continued. When a character's dialogue is interrupted by description, you should add (con't) following the character's name after the interruption. *Example:*

                    HARRY
        So, what shall we do? Can we . . .

    Harry picks up an old ashtray and turns it
    in his hands.

                    HARRY (con't)
        . . . pick up where we left off?

a) **MORE and CONTINUED:** When a character's entire dialogue can't be concluded on one page, center (MORE) under the dialogue at the bottom of the first page. At the top of the next page, write the character's name followed by (con't). *Example:*

First Page:

```
                    HARRY
    I'm scared, very scared. I don't

    know what's inside the thing, and

                    (MORE)
```

Second Page:

```
                    HARRY (con't)
        I just don't know what we're . . .
```

4. **Dueling Dialogue:** When two characters speak at the same time, their dialogue can be put on the page side by side; or, in the description, indicate that both characters speak at the same time, then place the chunks of dialogue one after the other.

5. **FADE IN/FADE OUT:** FADE IN is only used at the beginning of the script. FADE OUT is generally used only at the end. It is sufficient, but if you want to add or substitute THE END, you can do that.

6. **Flashbacks and Dream (or Fantasy) Sequences:** To indicate a dream or flashback sequence, treat them as scene headings by writing: BEGIN FLASHBACK or BEGIN DREAM SEQUENCE. Don't forget to end the sequence by writing: END FLASHBACK or END DREAM SEQUENCE or END FANTASY SEQUENCE.

7. **Montage:** A montage is indicated in the same manner as flashbacks. The shots to be included in the montage are usually listed with brief descriptions.

8. **Parenthetical:** This is material placed in parentheses immediately under a character's name, or in mid-dialogue if appropriate. It indicates how the line should be read.

9. **Phone Calls:** When two people are speaking together on the phone, it can be indicated either by cross-cutting between the two characters, or by having one character who is heard but not seen on screen. Generally, you follow the off-screen character's name with (ON THE PHONE) or (ON PHONE).

   Example:

HARRY (ON PHONE)
So, what do you say, Harriet?

10. **Scene Description:** This follows the scene heading and very briefly describes the scene and action.

11. **Scene Heading/Slug Line/Scene Slug:** This is the basic information at the beginning of each scene. It indicates if the scene is interior (INT.) or exterior (EXT.), where the scene is taking place, and what time of day it is.

12. **Sotto Voce and Ad Lib:** Sotto Voce means "under the breath." When you want a character to say something other characters can't hear, use (SOTTO VOCE) as a parenthetical. Use (AD LIB) to indicate when you want the actor(s) to create their own lines. Often used for background characters' scenes or when characters greet each other. Don't use it very often.

13. **Times of Day:** You don't have to specify anything more than DAY or NIGHT in your scene heading. If you want something more specific because it's important to your story, you can include it. Don't do it too often or be too specific unless it's crucial. If one scene immediately follows the previous one, you write: CONTINUOUS, FOLLOWING, or IMMEDIATELY AFTER. If a scene is happening in another place at exactly the same time as the previous scene, write AT THE SAME TIME or SIMULTANEOUSLY.

14. **Transitions:** This material indicates how the writer wants to move (cut, fade, dissolve, etc.) from one scene to another.

15. **V.O. and O.S.** When a character isn't on screen but is part of the scene you're writing, following the character's name above the dialogue, write (O.S.). When a character isn't really part of the scene but is "watching" or narrating it, following the character's name above the dialogue, write (V.O.).

THE BASICS

The following are the absolutes of proper formatting:

- Always write in present tense.

- Type the screenplay in Courier 12 point.

- Number the pages of your scripts.

- Begin with FADE IN. It's the equivalent of "Once upon a time."

THE FEATURE FILM FORMAT

Margins to Set: When setting your computer for writing your screenplay, set the margins to:

```
1 inch. . . . . . . . Top and bottom
11/2 inches. . . . . Left margin
1 inch. . . . . . . . Right margin
```

These margins apply to all but page one. On that sheet, you center the title at about an inch down from the top—a little more if you want, but not much. Include your name under the title.

Tabs to Set: Because the left and right margins are unequal, the entire layout is shifted to the right. Tabulations are measured from the left margin. Tabs are set as follows:

```
Flush to left margin . . . . . . . . . . . . . . . . . . . . . . . . . Scene heading/slug,
        camera suggestions, and scene descriptions
10–15 spaces from the left and right margins . . . . . . Dialogue
20–25 spaces from left margin . . . . . . . . . . . . . . . . Parentheticals
```

25–30 spaces from left margin .... Characters' names

55–60 spaces from left margin .... Transitions

What to Capitalize: The following terms are always capitalized in scripts:

BEGIN or END FLASHBACK/DREAM/FANTASY SEQUENCE
BEGIN MONTAGE/END MONTAGE
CAMERA DIRECTIONS
CHARACTERS' NAMES OVER DIALOGUE
CHARACTERS' NAMES WHEN FIRST INTRODUCED
FADE IN/FADE OUT
MORE/CONTINUED
SCENE HEADINGS/SLUGS/SLUGLINES
SOUND EFFECTS
THE END
TRANSITIONS
V.O./ O.S.

Single-Spacing: The following should be single-spaced:

Scene descriptions
Dialogue
Space between characters' names and their dialogue
Space between characters' names and parentheticals
Space between parenthetical directions and dialogue
Space between dialogue and (MORE) or (CON'T)

Double-Spacing: There are times when it's appropriate to double-space. They include:

Between scene headings and scene descriptions
Between scene descriptions and characters' names above dialogue
Between the last line of dialogue and what follows
Between FADE IN and the scene heading/slug
Between the last line in the script and FADE OUT
Between paragraphs of lengthy scene descriptions

Things That Don't Matter: Although new screenwriters fret and argue over many aspects of formatting, it just doesn't matter whether:

- You double- or triple-space between the end of one scene and the scene heading of a new scene.

- You use (con't) following a character's name after an interruption by a scene description. Some suggest not using it. Most scripts submitted to studios use it.

- You capitalize hand props. Some scripts do.

- You indent your dialogue, parenthicals, and character names the exact number of prescribed spaces—but it should hit close to the appropriate spot.

- You put quotation marks around the title of your script (it seems redundant) or if you capitalize the entire title on the first page of your work.

- You put a period after EXT and INT.

Beginning writers sometimes treat formatting as if each question were a life-and-death issue. Some rules are important, others less so. Don't agonize over the mechanical aspects of scriptwriting. Concentrate on creating a great story.

A SUGGESTION

Make sure there is plenty of "air" on your pages, i.e., white space. Strive for a good balance between scene description and dialogue (although it's not always possible). If you have a long action sequence to describe, break it up into short paragraphs. It's important.

SOME EXAMPLES

Following are two samples of script pages. The first indicates various script elements. The second is an example of a properly formatted script page that balances dialogue and description.

EXT. AN URBAN ALLEY – NIGHT (scene heading/slug/ scene slug)
(scene description) An Audrey-like plant sits next to
a huge, undented dumpster. The plant SNAPS up
insects. A BUM (all caps first time character is introduced)
wanders into the alley. He drops his fifth of
whiskey, cursing (AD LIB) when it breaks on the
pavement. He gets down and licks up the spilled
booze, cutting his tongue and pulling shards of
glass from his mouth.

(25-30 sp. from left margin)   DUMPSTER   (character name)
(20-25 sp. from left mar.)   (whispsering)   (parenthetical)
(10-15 sp. l. mar.) Wanna get rich?   (dialogue)

The bum looks at the dumpster uncomprehendingly.
Continues lapping up the whiskey.

                    DUMPSTER (con't)
          Don't miss this great opportunity.

                         BUM
          I'm talkin' to a dumpster?

                    DUMPSTER
          Your loss, pal. I've got a wallet
          in here with $20,000 in it.

                         BUM
          And I'd believe you 'cuz . . .

                    DUMPSTER
          Because it might be true.

The bum goes over to the bin. He cautiously opens
the lid and looks in. Opens it wider and leans in
farther. Then he loses his balance and falls in.

The lid SLAMS shut. The sounds of CHEWING followed
by a LIP SMACK, a loud BURP, and a SIGH of pleasure.

                    DUMPSTER
          Score!

                    AUDREY PLANT
          I get the next one.
                         (transition)   CUT TO:

Sample Script Page

EXT. A CLIFF PATH - LATE MORNING

VICTORIA, TAPPING a white cane, carefully walks
the cliff path. In the background, DESMOND shoots
out of the beach house and off the deck toward
her like an unguided missile.

> DESMOND
> (calling)
> Victoria!

Victoria stops and turns toward him.

> DESMOND (con't)
> What's this about firing Olivia?
> She says you fired her.

In the background, Olivia strolls languidly out
on the deck wearing an outfit J.Lo might be
embarrassed to wear.

> VICTORIA
> Desmond, please. I've been trying to
> talk to you about this for days. You
> won't even give me a minute.

Desmond reaches Victoria, out of breath.

> DESMOND
> I explained that.

> VICTORIA
> Some explanation!

> DESMOND
> So you're saying you fired Olivia
> because I didn't talk to you?

He turns and shares an exasperated look with
Olivia.

> VICTORIA
> I didn't fire her. Molly's
> returning. I no longer *need* her.

Title Pages: Title pages are supposed to be clean, neat, and quiet. They should be set up following this pattern:

TITLE OF WORK (all caps, centered)

by (double or triple space under title)

B.A. Starr

(author's name double/triple spaced under "by")

You can also use "An original screenplay by" or "A screenplay by." Some writers put quotation marks around the title. If you've adapted a book, that information should also be noted a few lines below the material shown above.

FORMATTING TELEVISION MOVIES

Television scripts use a distinct formatting approach that must be followed when writing material for that medium. Scripts for movies of the week are usually called "teleplays." The best approach is simply to format your material as you would a feature film. One difference between feature-film scripts and teleplays is length. MOWs usually run under 110 pages in order to fit a two-hour time block.

MOW shooting scripts are divided into seven acts that correspond to commercial breaks. But you needn't write them that way. If you do write in acts, keep in mind that act one is longer than the others because the first commercial break is at about eighteen to twenty-three minutes into the first hour. It's good to include a mini-cliffhanger at the end of each act for obvious reasons.

Remember: If you format with act breaks:

1. Start a new page for the beginning of each act.

2. Using all capitals and using words, not numbers, label each act, e.g., ACT ONE.

3. Some writers note the end of the act.

Hour-Long Formatting

Hour-long television shows are written in four acts, each about thirteen to fifteen pages long. They often include a teaser (no more than three or four pages long) at the beginning, and an epilogue (one or two pages long) at the end.

Formatting the hour-long is very simple. With the following exceptions, an hour-long is formatted as a feature film would be:

1. Label the beginning of each act, e.g., ACT ONE, etc.

2. Label the end of each act, e.g., END OF ACT ONE.

3. Use FADE IN and FADE OUT at the beginning and end of each act.

4. Act numbers and FADE IN/FADE OUT are written in all caps.

The First Page: About an inch and a half down from the top, double-space, center, underline, and capitalize:

1. The series name

2. The title of the episode

3. The act designation

Then drop down a couple of lines and begin your script.

The Title Page is pretty simple for hour-longs:

1. Capitalize and underline the name of the series.

2. Double-space below the series name, and capitalize and underline the title of your episode.

3. Come down several lines, then underline and write "Written" on one line, "by" on the next and your name on the next line (see example).

Following is an example of an hour-long television script's title and first pages.

Sample Title Page for an Hour-long

WELL DONE

THE GHOST IN THE MACHINE

Written

By

B. A. Starr

Your Name
Address
Contact Numbers

Sample Formatting for Hour-longs

WELL DONE
THE GHOST IN THE MACHINE
ACT ONE

FADE IN
EXT. THE HOSPITAL - NIGHT
An ambulance, SIREN wailing, pulls into
the emergency center and comes to a
SCREECHING halt. Two EMTs jump out . . .

INT. THE EMERGENCY ROOM - CONTINUOUS

Doctors come running . . .

FADE OUT

END OF ACT ONE

FORMATTING SITCOMS

Half-hour comedy series have their own format, which is quite dissimilar from that of feature films and hour-long television fare.

Half-hour shows are written in two acts. Sometimes a show has a final tag and/or a beginning teaser. The scene breaks within the acts occur each time the story or location shifts. The scenes are assigned letters, beginning with A.

For example, in an episode of *Scrubs*, Scene A might be in a hospital hallway. If a character goes into the emergency room, that becomes Scene B. One other note, parenthetical information is included more often in sitcoms than it is in other forms of screenwriting.

To Format Sitcoms, you should:

1. Capitalize and underline scene heading/slugs.

2. Capitalize and single-space scene descriptions.

3. Double-space after character's name above dialogue.

4. Double-space dialogue.

5. Put parentheticals at the beginning of the dialogue, not under the character's name.

6. Use FADE IN at the beginning of each act and the teaser (if the show has one).

7. Use CUT TO at the end of each scene and act.

8. Label the beginning of each act and each scene.

9. Act and scene labels are written out and capitalized.

10. In parentheses, write the scene letter under the page number (in the upper right-hand corner).

The First Page, which serves as the title page and sometimes the cover, includes:

1. The series name, capitalized and underlined.

2. Title of your episode, capitalized and, if you desire, in quotation marks.

3. The act, written out, capitalized and underlined.

4. Scene letter, capitalized and underlined.

At the beginning of each act and each new scene:

1. Start a fourth of the way down the page.

2. Center, cap, and underline ACT ONE or ACT TWO.

3. Down a couple lines, centered, underlined, and capped, place the scene letter: (<u>Scene A</u>) or (<u>A</u>)

4. About six or eight lines below the scene letter, begin the scene.

A sitcom sample page one follows:

<u>SHOW TITLE</u>
"NAME OF EPISODE"

<u>ACT ONE</u>
<u>A (Scene A)</u> <small>(can be written either way)</small>

FADE IN:
<u>INT. ALLEY - LATE AFTERNOON</u>
CHICK AND HAROLD ARRANGE A TRAY OF DELI-
CACIES FROM THE DISCARDED FOOD THEY PULL
OUT OF GARBAGE CANS.

                        CHICK
(ENGLISH ACCENT) I think we can
look forward to a sumptuous
feast tonight.
                                CUT TO:

12

The Camera, the Sound, and Your Screenplay

While you wrote your screenplay, you "saw" the scenes with your mind's eye. Sometimes you may even see the action in minute detail and from a particular point of view. For example: You write a scene of a couple of people meeting for the first time over coffee. You see them in a medium shot arriving at the restaurant and discovering each other. Your vision switches to a long shot across the restaurant as a waiter shows the two to a table. Move to a close-up of the two feeling uncomfortable and making awkward small talk. Easy? Not really. And, probably not necessary.

There is a 99 percent chance that if this script of yours is purchased, developed, and makes it to the local theaters, the vision on screen will resemble what runs through your head about as much as New York resemble Los Angeles.

This gap between what's in your head and what eventually appears on screen is one of the reasons writers often want to direct their own films. But here's the next catch. Even when you direct your own material, chances are that the ultimate screen version will have little in common with what's playing in your head as you write the script.

There are many reasons why this happens. For example, all the camera angles in the preceding scene aren't necessary. The angles are *implied* by the action. Only the most clueless director and DP could miss the shots.

The other reasons have everything to do with money—the ruling force inside the borders of Cinema City. Money rules just about every decision made regarding everything, from above-the-line people down through the temporary PAs, i.e., production assistants.

You can't help getting these pictures in your head; your imagination is so visually based that they won't stop coming. And hey, that's why you're writing screenplays instead of obscure novels or papers on probability theory. Don't try to stop the images. Let them come, let them lead you; otherwise it's not nearly so much fun to write.

It might be that by the time the script you're working on is sold and put into production, you'll be so old you'll be going to an Alzheimer's twelve-step program to figure out ways to remember who you are and how to find your way home. A script you wrote years and years earlier will be an irretrievable memory. Or, less depressingly and more realistically, you will be four or five scripts removed from the one getting produced and you won't remember specific images. When the director decides to set the scene in a Denny's outside El Paso, shot exclusively in two shots at midday, you won't remember your original vision—the Ritz in Paris, filmed in long, medium, and close-up shots, each suffused with sensuous afternoon sunlight.

If neither of these eventualities occurs, and if it happens that you get the work you've hurled from your imagination to the screen before you've forgotten what you wrote, be prepared to wince. What you see on the big screen won't match what you saw in your head. The point of view won't duplicate what you envisioned, the actors won't read the lines as you imagined hearing them, and the timing and placement of the shots will all deviate significantly from what you envisioned.

Unless you have the opportunity to take part in each and every stage of the production, and budget is of no concern, be prepared for surprises. But think for a minute. How often has someone described something to you, but when you actually experienced the thing described, it was completely different from what you expected? Remember the last blind date you had? Did you ever look at a rental house you saw described in the want ads? Okay, you get the point. But how can you get as close as possible to having your script's images reproduced in the final product?

Try to get yourself involved in the production. That's not always easy, and sometimes it's disastrous. Too often production companies want to dispense with the writer ASAP. It seems a cruel thing to do, to ignore a resource who could be a great help. But it's done all the time. No one will pay the writer any mind, even if he or she is on the set. Usually no one wants the writer around for various reasons.

There's ego, of course. In this case it's often the director's. He regards the script as raw material upon which he will imprint his own style, ideas, visions, and philosophies, ad infinitum nauseam. You would think the director created this material himself, just as later the audiences will think the actors are making up the dialogue they repeat for the camera.

It isn't always bad that the director takes possession of the material and makes it his own. Often a director can take material and make it something more wonderful than it was originally.

Sometimes the director, producer, and crew don't want the screenplay's author around because the writer will whine about the many ways the production is deviating from the original conception, which he, by this time, has come to regard as second in importance only to those two stone slabs Moses found freshly carved on Sinai. So the writer, with his gnashing of teeth, constant tears, contrary attitude, and discontent, becomes a drag on the process. Everyone eventually wants to get him on a flight to somewhere deep in Uzbekistan where the roads have been washed out since Marco Polo came through.

Short of becoming a real producer-writer, someone who will be on the set and do meaningful work as opposed to someone who's a producer in name only ("producer" being a Hollywood title that's apparently handed out to anyone who has the temerity to ask for it), you have to do your best to convey as much information as possible that can be understood by a director, cinematographer, art director, and others on the crew. Later on, when you're directing your own material, or at least having some input as a producer-writer, you may not need the following information. But for now, the following terms will help you communicate with the people who will be molding your work for the big screen.

THE SHOOTING

The following terms shouldn't be overused. Give the DP a little credit; he may know better than you how to shoot a particular scene so that it will have the impact you intended. That goes for the director, too. Give him credit for understanding the emotional center of a scene and supplying a few ideas of how to reach it successfully, even if it isn't shot the way you wrote it. Let them do their work; don't overload them with instruction. More often than not, scripts are written without any camera shots indicated. However, sometimes you will determine that a scene calls for a specific shot—you figure it is the only way to communicate the information you want conveyed in the scene. A sensible approach is to save the very specific instructions for a few crucial scenes.

CAMERA ANGLES

Whether or not you decide to use camera instructions, it's probably a good idea to know them. And if you decide to use them, remember, *don't overdo it.*

Establishing Shot

This is a long shot coming at the beginning of a film or a scene that establishes the time and place of the action and can also convey the tone. *Night Moves* opened with a shot that follows a not-very-expensive car down a semi-seedy street dotted with small businesses and stays with it as it the car is parked in front of a shabby building. A large man, dressed in very ordinary casual clothing, gets out and goes into an office. The viewer knows immediately where this fellow belongs on the social scale, where he is on the ladder of success, and the nature of his physical surroundings. Even if you start your film in a tight, close shot, at some point you have to let the audience know where they are. *The Village* introduced us immediately to three young women who looked as if they belonged perhaps in the mid-1800s. As they strolled through the village, we saw a typical small town of that era. We learned everything we needed to know to locate ourselves in this story.

Long Shot

This is a relative term, but a long shot is usually taken from far enough away that it includes the landscape or a building or a large exterior. How many times in *Die Hard* was the full shot of the building used? That's a long shot. The shots of the police, the FBI, and various other law-enforcement people who gathered at the foot of the building are also long shots.

Medium Shots

Basically there are three types of medium shots. A medium-close shot is from the mid-chest up. A mid-shot cuts the figures off just below the waist, and a medium shot is from below the knee up. You don't have to be this specific.

Close-Up or Close Shot

A close shot ranges from shots taken of a subject from the chest up to having the character's face fill the screen. A close-up is called for if you want the subject of the shot to fill the entire screen, e.g., the car, the dog, the gun. You get the idea.

These are the basic four shots. But there are others that get more specific and should be used sparingly and with care.

Extreme Long Shot

Remember the shots across the city from the hillsides of Los Angeles in *Mulholland Falls*? They are extreme long shots. They are also termed "wide angle shots" in some cases.

Extreme Close-Up

If a close-up shows the subject's head and top of his shoulders, then an extreme close-up shows just his face. If it's important for the audience to see something, like, say, the key in *Notorious*, the stolen money in *Psycho*, or a reaction shot, then you want to do a close-up. But if the condition of the object, or its characteristics, or a small movement, like a squint or a blink, is important, then include an extreme close-up.

Full Shot

In this shot, the subject (human figure or an object) is entirely in the frame. In *Miss Congeniality 2*, Sandra Bullock's character is shown in full shot, from head to toe, after she completes her months-long beauty and style redo. The audience needs to see that the newly remodeled FBI agent, known for her sloppiness and lack of social and grooming skills, has now become a poised fashionista.

Two Shot

This shot includes two figures. It is probably not really necessary to specify this when you put the finishing touches on your script because it will be obvious from the scene you're writing that there are two and only two characters in the shot.

Three Shot and One Shot

Same as the previous description except, well, you've already figured it out.

Over-the-Shoulder Shot

This is usually a two or three shot in which the camera is placed behind the shoulder of one of the characters and favors (focuses on) the other character.

Point-of-View Shot

This is a useful shot to include in your screenplay if the audience needs to see what a particular character sees. Again, in *Miss Congeniality 2*, Sandra Bullock's character sees what she thinks is a Dolly Parton impersonator. When she spots her, so does the audience, as we see the action from her POV.

Low-Angle Shot

In this shot, the camera is set low and is angled up on the action. Oftentimes this is combined with a point-of-view shot so that the character seeing everything from below feels small, intimidated, frightened, or overpowered. In *Space Cowboys*, for example, a low angle of the rocket that will launch the overaged crew creates a sense of importance and suggests how powerful, expensive, awesome, and slightly frightening this piece of machinery is, with its slick lines and ominous steam. The shot can be employed in mysteries or thrillers to confer a menacing quality to whatever it is that the character is looking up at. It is also often used to convey a child's or small animal's perspective in a scene.

High-Angle Shot

This is the reverse of a low-angle shot. The camera is tilted down on what is being photographed. The psychological implications are the reverse of the low-angle shot. In *The Third Man*, Harry Lime (Orson Welles) takes his friend Holly Martins (Joseph Cotten) on a Ferris wheel ride. When they reach the highest point of the arc, he looks down on the people—"the dots," he calls them—walking around below, and ponders on their importance. If your character is powerful or haughty or holds himself above the masses, this may be a good angle to occasionally employ—it magnifies the character's importance.

Insert Shot

This is used when we need to see something that is or will be important to the story. The old chestnut here is the clock face. If your characters must synchronize their watches, often an insert of a watch face—it fills the screen—is included. If a character finds an object, say, like a bracelet, and realizes it's the one that was stolen earlier, an insert shot is used to reveal to the audience that this is the exact same bracelet. Insert shots are so called because they can be photographed by the second unit and inserted into the film in the editing room.

Scripts use a shorthand for camera shots. Instead of writing them out, especially when using mediums, two shots, and full and long shots, often the writer will simply put ANOTHER ANGLE or ANGLE ON followed by what the camera will focus on. This indicates a shift in the scene and at the same time allows the director of photography to employ his skills and art to determine the particular shot for this scene.

CAMERA MOVEMENT

There are a variety of ways to employ camera movement to tell your story.

Aerial Shot

This is an exterior shot taken from a plane or a helicopter. If you want the audience to feel the vastness of the landscape or see a large piece of action at once, use this shot. In chase scenes, aerial shots allow the audience to get a sense of the complete action.

Crane Shot

The camera is put on a special movable crane. From this vantage point, it can follow the action's various directions. In *The Wild Bunch*, the shootout between the men and the railroad officials includes several crane shots.

Dolly, Tracking, Trucking Shots

In these shots, the camera moves alongside the subject of the scene, toward or away from the subject, or along with the subject as the character walks toward or away from the camera. The shots can be taken from a vehicle (a car, truck, train, etc.), from a camera on a Steadicam, or from tracks on which the camera is mounted. Many times this kind of shot is assumed. For example, if you have two characters walking down a street talking to each other, tracking is implied, and noting the type of shot to be done isn't necessary.

Pullback Dolly

This is a camera movement that is used to reveal something to the audience that was previously off screen. It's often used in thrillers or mysteries. The character on screen sees something important off screen. It's only after the character reacts to it that the camera pulls back and the audience gets to see what the character saw.

Pan, Panning Shot

The "pan" is short for "panorama." In this shot, the camera moves horizontally from left to right or right to left around a vertical axis. It's often used in establishing shots. Remember *Patton*? There were dozens of pan shots in that film. This shot goes with epic films like vermouth goes with gin.

Swish Pan

This shot is also called a "flash" or "zip pan." It is a horizontal movement, sometimes 360 degrees, around a vertical axis at such a high rate of speed that the picture becomes a blur. *Snake Eyes* has an example. In one scene, Rick Santoro (Nicolas Cage) is in a casino, where he searches for a culprit by quickly scanning the area. His POV is a swish pan around the entire arena. Swish shots are usually of very short duration. They are meant to be rapid, dizzying shots or simply to duplicate the rapid movement of the human eye. When they end, many times the story has shifted to a new location.

Tilt Shot

This shot is the vertical version of the pan shot. In this shot, the camera moves up and down around a horizontal axis. It isn't used as often as the pan, but it has its place. The tilt shot is often used when a male character spots a beautiful woman and looks her over from her toes to her head. The camera tilts has the man's eyes move upward. It's a POV tilt shot.

THROUGH THE LENS

Indicting particular approaches to the quality of a shot is a third way to insure that your vision is conveyed more precisely to a film crew.

Fish-Eye Lens

There's a very good chance you will never use this particular designation in your script. Basically, it's an extremely wide-angle lens that distorts the image so severely that it appears curved. Only if your characters are on drugs, drunk, or mentally disturbed might you use this. Or if you're doing a music video.

Freeze Frame

A single frame of film is reprinted a number of times so that when it's projected, the image appears to be a still photograph. It's often used at the end of films behind the credit roll and is actually an editing technique, although many times the image gradually becomes a blur, which can be done by manipulating the lens or in the cutting room.

Rack Focus

If you've ever seen a shot in a movie in which the foreground is in focus and the background out of focus, or a face on one side of the screen is in focus while the face on the other side of the screen isn't, then you've seen rack focus. A writer might call for rack focus if something on screen needs to be emphasized, after which the audience's focus needs to be redirected to another part of the screen.

Soft Focus

Soft focus is the blurring of everything in the scene except the object of the shot or one plane in the depth of field. Sometimes every part of the frame is blurry. It can create a romantic feel or indicate an indistinct memory or a character becoming conscious, or it can indicate that nothing but the object of the scene, which is in focus, is being watched or is important.

Split Screen

In the 1950s and early 1960s, when characters spoke by phone on screen, the filmmakers often opted to show both characters by using the split screen. The recent *Down with Love* used this technique. This film, inspired by the 1959 film *Pillow Talk*, hoped to capture the earlier film's style through the use of this technique, which is rarely employed by contemporary filmmakers. The original *The Thomas Crown Affair* gained a bit of critical notice for its playful use of this technique. It was one of the first films to feature simultaneous actions by cutting the screen into multiple frames. This style can currently be seen regularly on the television series *24*.

Zoom Shot

If you've watched television in the last twenty years, or bought a camera in the last few years, you're already familiar with zooming in or zooming out of scenes.

The lens has variable focus lengths and without moving the camera, we can get closer to the action by zooming in on the scene and then move away from it by zooming back out. Use it sparingly in scriptwriting. It is used occasionally when characters spot something or someone they have been searching for and their eyes "zoom" in.

SOUND

There may be times when you need to indicate how the sound works with what the audience sees on screen. The following describes how to indicate how you want sound to work in your screenplay. Use these instructions sparingly and have good dramatic justification for their inclusion.

MOS

This is one of the most famous abbreviations in film. MOS are the initials for "mit out sound," a kind of mangled combination of German and English. It means "without sound." If you want one of your scenes to play without the audience hearing the dialogue, or if you want it completely silent, then you need to indicate on the script that it is an MOS scene.

Off Screen

If you have a character who is in the scene but is not on screen, you use (O.S.) above his or her dialogue following the character's name. Some writers use O.C. for off camera, but O.S. is more common.

Sound Effects

Sound effects, such as window glass being smashed or fire-engine sirens, are added to the film after the shooting is complete. It's usually indicated by capitalizing the sound effects you need in a scene. For example:

```
INT. A FARM - DAY
Jimmy trudges from the barn to the farm-
house weighed down by two buckets of milk.
Chickens CLUCK and CROW, cows MOO, and a
dog BARKS as the 12-year-old goes across
the porch and through the screen door,
letting it SLAM behind him.
```

The sounds indicated above would be added in the post-production sound editing. If you have written a scene in which lots of sounds are heard simultaneously, you might want to note it in the easiest possible way, such as: Appropriate SFX for Times Square on New Year's Eve.

Synchronous and Nonsynchronous Sound

"Synchronous" means that the image and sound are recorded simultaneously, or appear to be. The sound matches the action on screen. Nonsynchronous includes the music score and background sounds. But you don't indicate background music by using the above term. You just indicate the music you want behind the action and/or dialogue you've written. Synchronous sound is implied and needs no notation.

Voiceover

The proper way to indicate you're using a narrator for a scene is by capitalizing the character's name and following it with (V.O.) above the voiceover dialogue. This sound will also be added in post.

Now then, if you go back through your script and add the notations we've just covered, where appropriate, the scenes that you've pulled from your head and put on the page will be one step closer to being realized on screen.

13

Help from Your Computer

Today's writers may have it too easy. Help for struggling writers is as nearby as your computer. Logging on to one of the many Web sites that provide aid and information to screenwriters hoping to succeed in Hollywood cuts down the time and effort research requires and eliminates a lot of the second- or sixtieth-hand information that writers in remote locations had to depend on to guide their work.

There are dozens and dozens of sites with information for writers on screenplay development and format; locating seminars and workshops; finding supplies, books, and needed materials;

entering competitions; and finding appropriate schools. Web sites also offer interviews with the authors of current films, development executives, authors of books about screenwriting, script analysts, and others considered relevant to the subject.

THE NET

"Old-school" in Internet years means the pages of a Web site have been up and operating for more than five years. Following, then, are these firmly established addresses:

- *http://wga.org/writtenby*: This is the site of the Writers Guild and its magazine, *Written By.* You will find a lot of Guild material here directed specifically at writers and the issues they face in writing and selling scripts. This site also provides links to writers' software programs. You're sure to find something here that will interest or help you.

- *www.script-o-rama.com*: At Drew's Script-O-Rama you can download film or television scripts for no charge. There are also other offerings and links to other sites that writers might find worth a look.

- *www.scriptdude.com*: Story planners, scripts, format information, brainstorming ideas, and story planner software demos are all included at the Scriptdude Web page. If you want to preview and/or buy a scriptwriting program, this spot can be helpful.

- *www.screenwritersutopia.com*: Links to writing software are among the payoffs at Screenwriter's Utopia.

- *www.wordplayer.com*: An unassuming little site that also offers aid and comfort to writers. It offers much the same information for writers as do other sites, it just does it with fewer graphics and less clutter.

There are many other places writers can visit to find out what's going on in the profession of screenwriting. The following list isn't all-inclusive but represents the more prominent sites. This list also includes the e-zine version of the screenwriting magazines listed in another chapter in this book. All the sites feature information on contests, interviews, links to other sites, articles on screenwriting, helpful hints, and maybe more information than you can handle at one sitting:

- *www.absolutewrite.com*: Absolute Write offers workshops, interviews, and miscellaneous information on their site as well as in their newsletter.

- *www.creativescreenwriting.com*: This site is the online version of the *Creative Screenwriting* magazine.

- *www.filmmakers.com*: Film*Makers* is another magazine to check out. The page that lists various screenplay contests is updated frequently.

- *www.firstwriter.com*: First Writer contains details and contact information on hundreds of screenwriting competitions.

- *www.inktip.com*: Here you can post your screenplays and loglines for a fee. It also offers tips for writers and a newsletter.

- *www.moviemaker.com/hop*: Listings of upcoming workshops and speakers can be found at the MovieMaker Hands On Pages. This site is *MovieMaker* magazine's online version. It also includes all the usual material that the other magazines offer.

- *www.onlinefmc.com*: Filmmaker's Central offers information on filmmaking workshops.

- *www.pitchfest.com*: This site offers information on the annual The Great American PitchFest festival held in Los Angeles each spring.

- *www.scriptjournal.com*: Script Journal presents information on upcoming workshops and seminars in addition to the standard fare.

- *www.scriptpimp.com*: Calling itself the "pipeline into motion pictures," it runs competitions, notice of workshops, and other news and products.

- *www.scriptshark.com*: Offers a variety of information and products.

- *www.scriptmag.com*: This is the online address for *scr(i)pt* magazine. It focuses on interviews with writers of current flicks, workshop information, and contests.

- *www.soyouwannasellascript.com*: The focus of this site is on screenwriting competitions.

There are many, many sites on the Web whose purpose is to serve screenwriters. Maybe there are too many; once you begin a search, it can become overwhelming. So many contests, so many interviews, so many writing tips—it might make you rethink the entire effort. When you feel like you are suffering from information overload, it's time to log off and refocus on your own work.

The above information isn't a testament to the worthiness of the sites, it is just that these magazines and sites have been around a while and are pretty credible and reliable.

MORE NOTABLE NET SPOTS

Beyond the sites devoted exclusively to screenwriting or screenplays, there are other sites that can supply you with helpful information about films and the business of making movies.

The dull-sounding but often-visited and data-heavy Internet Movie Database (IMDb) site has a storehouse of information on thousands of films. Want to know who released a particular film? It's there. Want a list of credits for a particular film? It's there. Want to know how much money a film made? It's there. This place is a real fount of down-to-earth, solid information. There's even a page of gossip and a page of goofs for most films. Their address is *www.imdb.com*.

To access the *Hollywood Creative Directory*, go to *www.hcdonline.com*. Log on, subscribe, and keep current about production companies doing business in Hollywood.

Another page that offers solid information on movies is the Box Office Guru. Here you'll find all sorts of statistics about the movies made since 1997. Don't look for gossip here. Find them at *www.boxofficeguru.com*.

A less formal approach to movie information can be found at Ain't It Cool News (*www.aintitcool.com*). Here you can get an update on the current status of an ongoing television series, upcoming movies, and those in current release, as well as celebrity news and gossip, if there's any difference between those two anymore.

The Hollywood Film Festival site (*www.hollywoodawards.com*) may be worth a look. The tone is a little more highbrow than many other sites. In addition to the information offered about the Festival, the site sponsors the Cinema Salon (*www.hollywoodawards.com/worldcinema.html*). Films can be submitted for screening at ArcLight Cinemas, the former Pacific Theatres' Cinerama Dome on Sunset Boulevard.

If you're looking for straightforward news about the film and television industry, you can find it at either *www.variety.com* or *www.hollywoodreporter.com*. These are the Web versions of the daily trade newspapers. If you want the complete version, you have to subscribe online, but there's lots of stuff that's free to read, like current movies' box-office results.

Hollywood Online (*www.hollywood.com*) offers a movie guide, a studio store, show times for theaters in your area, and box-office results. It also runs features on movie celebs.

The studios haven't let this particular technology pass them by. All of them are represented on the Web. Naturally, they provide a menu of all their various business lines, information about their latest offerings, products you can buy, and other information. Most upcoming film releases also establish their own Web page. The Internet Movie Database (*www.imdb.com*) is an excellent resource for finding a movie's official Web page. You can also try typing the movie's name followed by "-themovie.com" into your Web browser.

WRITING SOFTWARE

Writing software falls into two main categories: those that lead writers through the steps of creating plot and characters, and those that format the script properly as you write it. Writers who have used software develop a favorite, and when you try a couple programs, you will too.

Final Draft

This formatting software has almost become the standard. It is very user-friendly, and the instruction booklet isn't written in technogeek-speak. The program offers lots of features and refinements. Go through the tutorial in the book and follow along. You can get the basics down pretty quickly, and then you can move on to learning the additional options. Final Draft offers a great thesaurus and dictionary.

This program also offers Final Draft AV for audiovisual scripts and Final Draft Scriptwriter's Suite, which includes both the screenplay and audiovisual software.

Movie Magic Screenwriter

"Magic" is the other big dog on the block of formatting. It too is easy to use and doesn't take much time to get used to. It keeps track of all characters and other elements you've written, such as settings, so that the second time you refer to it, the information is automatically typed. It also features an index card page. Here you can see your scenes in various configurations—as four, six, or nine cards.

It includes formats for film, television, or stage. Movie Magic Screenwriter is a story program that helps writers who get stuck in their work or want help forming it.

Other Programs for Screenwriters

- **Hollywood Screenwriter**: This is another program that provides proper formatting for your script.

- Software that helps you develop your story include **Fiction Master** for the more advanced writer and **TotallyWrite Development Suite** to help you with plot and characterization problems.

- **FirstAid for Writers**: This software is less specific than a formatting program, but it promises to strengthen or jump-start your work by helping with story and writing problems.

- **Power Tracker**: This marketing program offers strategies and tips for writers to "go out there and make it happen."

Formatting software is no longer a choice. The job of putting the story on paper is simply so much easier with software that most writers don't know how they did it before the programs were available. If you haven't already purchased such software, you will want to check out all the preceding materials to find a program that works for you.

14

Is It a Screenplay if No One Sees It but You?

Congratulations! You're done. After three weeks, three months, or three years, you have finished your screenplay. You have completed a big job. Don't let anyone tell you differently. You've lived through the highs and the lows of creating it; you probably thought a time or two that you wouldn't finish. But that is all past. It's done.

Now what? You might want to take a little R & R. Set aside your screenplay for a few days. Let it cool. It will help you be more objective when you go back to it. And you will go back to it, even if at this moment you can't bear to look at it. You have lived it and breathed it and rolled around in it for a long time and now you want and need a break. Take it.

The script will call you soon enough and demand to be dealt with again. It's a good thing it will, because you aren't finished with it yet, even if you think you are. You aren't. You just finished one of the two most significant steps of a multistep process.

THE POST-BREAK REVIEW

After a week or two or three, or maybe even more, go back to your desk and take out your opus. It's time to get the thing in fighting shape.

Read through it slowly and carefully. You need to see how it feels to you. Does it sound like what you had in mind when you first started on this story? Does the story flow as you had imagined it would? Does it seem sluggish, slow, senseless, confusing, confined, and superficial? Or are you still in love with everything you wrote, down to each period and dialogue beginning with "Well . . ."? If you still love it all, maybe you need to give it more time to rest. If you can see nothing that needs improving, maybe what you need is another point of view. That will come inevitably, after the first major revision.

YOU SAID IT, NOW TAKE IT BACK

If this is your first script and your first serious, extensive writing project, there is a good chance you took this opportunity to get everything that was on your chest, in your mind, and weighing on your heart down on paper. In fact, wanting to express all your thoughts is a strong motivating force to work through a 100- to 120-page story.

Bad news: The first step in rewriting your work will probably involve you excising a lot of your personal ruminations. One sure sign of a first-timer is a script that's more political, philosophical, sociological, or religious diatribe than story. When a story's characters are nothing more than mouthpieces for the author's point of view, a script is in trouble.

Does that mean that movies shouldn't take a particular political stance? Absolutely not. Open the newspaper to the movie/television section and you'll see writers' ideas about life spread all over. If you ever saw the films of John Sayles and movies made from the books of Nick Hornby, then you've seen writers who have filled stories with their personal views on various topics. However, they told us stories with characters who behaved as we might expect ordinary people to behave. The stories revolved around people who had to deal with the issues raised by the film. If the scripts of these films had had characters lecturing each other, or had they lectured the audience about the topic, the theaters would have emptied out in a flash.

If you have undergirded your exciting and thoughtful screenplay with gems of wisdom, that is a fabulous achievement for a first script. Experience has shown, however, that first-timers need to get all that stuff off their minds, then go back through the work and dump most of it out. Incorporate the rest within the context of the main story, and get on with refining it.

BE MERCILESS

Every writer rewrites, even the most famous. Vladimir Nabokov claimed he rewrote every word he had ever written. Ernest Hemingway, an earthier sort, expressed his views with, "The first draft of anything is shit." Of course, not all writers rewrite every single thing, but rewriting is a part of the job. Nine times out of ten, your work will be improved by rewriting it at least, at the very least, once.

So, after you scrape off the excessive philosophical musings and disgruntled ravings, face your story squarely and determine that you're going to shape it up. Determine what must go. Look at the length of your screenplay. If you're over 125 pages, you most certainly must cut. And you can. Analysts understand what you are describing even if you use three, six, or twenty fewer words to tell us about it. More importantly, go back through the dialogue. You probably will find that you've repeated yourself and explained too much in your characters' speeches. It can be cut. Get your characters' dialogue down to three or four lines and, in many cases, less. Check the script for typos and grammatical errors. If you feel unsure of yourself in this area, get out that copy of Strunk and White's *The Elements of Style* you just bought; it's been the authority on good writing forever. Fix all that you find. There will be other errors you will miss. It is crucial that the first page be *flawless*, absolutely flawless. It's the first-impression page. If it is sloppy, error-ridden, or placed on the page incorrectly, the analyst, the producer, and the reader—any reader—will despair.

After you've finished the obvious things, go back through and rethink your story. Is it excessively straightforward? Think of how you can take some unexpected detours and still find your way home by FADE OUT. Does it flow logically? Does it make any sense? Is it interesting? Have we seen stories very similar to yours on TV about a thousand times? What makes yours different? Anything? If not, give it something different. Do you have any subplots? How do they work with the primary plot? Are your act climaxes clear, and do they turn the story?

Now take a look at your characters and give each of them a grilling. At each stage in the story, in each scene in which a character is faced with alternative choices, why does the character make the decision he or she makes? What other decisions might the character make? You need to go back and reacquaint yourself with your characters. They don't just exist to make your plot work. You can't have them running hither and yon just because the plot demands it. They have rights, they have personalities, and they often have minds of their own. They'll help you write, or in this case rewrite, your script if you give them a little freedom. Once you really get to know them, you'll probably want to change more dialogue, only this time, it will be change that flows out of the character's personality.

You may rewrite two, three, or more times, plus do some tweaking here and there. You will know when you're done—when it feels complete. If you ignore this feeling and keep playing with your work, it might be because you hesitate to take the next step in the process.

GET IT OUT THERE

Move into the next phase slyly and obliquely by first fixing the format one last time. When you are completely finished, make a brand-new, never-been-touched, cleaner-than-clean copy and set it on your desk. Gaze upon your baby with pride. It's all dressed up and ready to go. It needs to be at its best. The next steps are difficult ones. Not every writer chooses to do this, but many do, and it can be very helpful to new writers: Ask someone to read it.

Start easy here. Ask a friend. A buddy probably can't give you any professional criticism, unless your friend it happens to be William Goldman or Linda Seger, but by starting out asking a good friend, you have time to get used to the idea of some-one reading your words. When your friend reports back to you, listen between the lines. If he says he missed something early on and so didn't understand something at the end, or if he really hated a character you meant to be likable, then you've got some criticism without your friend knowing he helped you.

If you're in a writing group, ask one of the members to read your work. She can give you new insights to the story. So far, you've controlled the universe you created on paper and things have worked pretty much the way you designed them. But another reader coming from a whole different sensibility can see your work in a light you never considered. That alternative outlook can help strengthen it.

After getting responses from acquaintances you have asked to read your work, decide which are valid criticisms and which say more about your acquain-tances than they do about your screenplay. For example, maybe a friend will tell you he hated your main character because he was a drunk. That kind of comment probably says more about your friend and what he is and is not sympathetic to. If you wrote your whole story around a character who's a drunk, that was your intention, and this criticism can be taken with a grain of salt. If, however, the reader said he hated the character because he was a drunk who didn't change or deal with that, then maybe your friend missed the redemption scene. That can mean that it wasn't strongly and clearly written. You need to take a look at it.

If you have contacts with theater groups, actors, drama teachers and their students, or even good readers, it can be an extremely helpful exercise to have them read your work.

Doing a reading or a readers' theater presentation of your work will let you see immediately what dialogue doesn't work, what sings, and what runs counter to the characters you've created. The holes in the plot will glare at you.

If you decide to get people together to perform your work orally, the best of all possible worlds is finding professional actors and a director. Good theater directors can see possibilities in your work that you're probably unaware of. They can bring a fresh approach and new insights to it.

If getting the services of a professional director isn't a possibility, there are other options. If you know someone with directing experience or an experienced actor, it will be to your advantage to ask them to read.

If you're going to rely on friends who've agreed to read your work, give them copies ahead of time and encourage them to read through it, or at least to read their lines several times so they can get a feel for the story and the characters. Consider asking people you know to attend the reading and listen to the performance. They too can give you helpful feedback.

Obtaining the services of someone with knowledge of screenwriting, story-telling, and character building to look at the script will also aid you in your quest to make your work the best it can be. A professional story analyst will cost you some bucks, but it will be worth it. Analysts who have worked in the film business for some time understand what is required for a screenplay to succeed.

There are a couple of considerations to remember here. The analyst should critique your story as a story and also estimate your work's chances of impressing Hollywood. Perhaps your screenplay is very familiar; it's a story that's been done to death. But the analyst knows if there is always a market for this particular kind of material and will determine whether you have put a fresh enough twist on it.

For example, think of all the buddy movies you've seen. From *It Happened One Night* to *Sideways*, this genre has been worked and reworked. The reason *Stuck On You* got made was because it is a new twist on a standard genre. Got a new take on vampire movies? On comic-book or graphic-novel material? On extraterrestrials—mineral, vegetable, or animal—threatening the earth? Remember, no one was interested in making *Star Wars* back in the 1970s.

The analyst might see a story well told, unique, and clever. Perhaps your story isn't high concept. Perhaps it's a terrific story but the lead character is a middle-aged or older man or woman, or it is about someone with a terminal disease. Hollywood knows that such stories rarely sell many tickets. So, despite your fine work, you will probably have a struggle on your hands to sell it. The upside is that good writing gets you noticed even if the script that shows it off isn't bought or produced.

CRITIQUES

Hearing your work and getting comments can be pretty scary, especially if you're inexperienced. When you write, you lay yourself, or some part of yourself, bare. Every writer experiences it. Committing something to paper, something from your heart, moves you from entertainment consumer to entertainer. Your work is out there for everyone to see and judge.

Criticism is never easy to take. Even experienced writers struggle with it. You feel, at the least, a little wounded. That's another reason why it's good to get some distance from your work—if it isn't fresh and raw, you can view negative reactions with more dispassion. When you are on the receiving end of critical analysis, you secretly decide that everyone who said anything negative is an insensitive idiot who understands nothing. But deep inside, one of those sprites, those goblins who plagued you all the way through, chuckles malevolently and whispers, "You're the idiot." It's enough to make you reach for the Jack Daniel's.

Give it a little time. Sometimes an hour or two takes off the sting. Sometimes, by the next day, the criticism looks pretty valid and suddenly you have some new ideas to make this terrific work even better. You're on your way again. After more rewrites, you will know when it's time to start showing your baby to possible adopters.

There's something you should keep in mind: It's human nature, heaven knows why, to remember the unkind rather than the complimentary comment. Strive to remember the positive. Both positive and negative are equally valid, or invalid, as the case may be. And while you're hurting, remember how much you can learn from the negative responses. The negative makes you grow, the positive gives you courage.

PUTTING THE WHOLE PACKAGE TOGETHER

Your efforts have got you to the screenplay you want, the one you're ready to show. But. Yes, there is a but. You have a few other items to finish before you log on to Inktip.com or dial Dreamworks' number.

Almost anyone you contact, whether it's a producer, a story executive, an agent, or a manager, will undoubtedly ask that you send a synopsis or some shortened form of your work before they'll look at the script itself. So warm up your computer—you have more writing to do.

Logline

Remember the premise you wrote and polished before you began your screenplay? Is it still applicable to your finished work? Even if it continues to capture your story, you will probably want to hone and rewrite to transform it into a true logline. As noted earlier, a logline is the shorthand used in the business that quickly identifies the content of a script. Sometimes it is the only material communicated about your screenplay. For example, in story meetings, analysts will read the logline to see if anyone is intrigued by the story line or genre or analysts will speak of a script by referring only to its title and logline. If that isn't intimidating enough, scripts often drown or float on this description alone. So, exactly what is it? A logline is a one- or two-sentence summary of your material—a refined, abbreviated premise.

Take note: A logline is not, repeat, not the film's theme or its symbolic meaning or a summary of the philosophical point of view expressed in the story. It is simply what the story is about. What is the question raised by the story, and who has to do what to answer it? What action is promised, and what will we see on screen? For example: A none-too-bright but likable goofball is forced to take over his father's brake manufacturing plant, save it for the town, and prevent his new stepbrother from gaining control of it after his father dies. Recognize this? Yes, it's *Tommy Boy*. The question raised by the story is, can Tommy Boy succeed?

Here's another: After being hypnotized, a young man who has an emotionally and mentally hateful job disengages from his work, and with two fellow unhappy coworkers, he schemes to defraud the company. This film, as you probably already know, is *Office Space*.

Here's one: An obsessive-compulsive reclusive writer, whose communication skills are a shambles, becomes "socialized" and finds love after he aids the waitress who serves him at the café he patronizes, and after he's forced to interact with his neighbor. You know this movie too; it's *As Good as It Gets*.

How do you write loglines? In no more than one or two sentences, reveal the protagonist of your story and what he or she has to achieve over the course of the film. Don't include information on subplots. Don't include the back story of your hero, just an identifying characteristic or two (likable goofball, obsessive-compulsive reclusive). Don't include all the complications that will arise in act two. Naturally, you will want to make the movie sound as exciting and engaging as you can in this very brief description.

The Summary

If you have piqued the interest of a producer, you will usually be asked to send a one- or two-paragraph summary of your screenplay along with your logline. From this, producers will decide whether they want to read the script.

Writing a short summary can be a challenge in more ways than one. For many writers, being brief and succinct is a struggle—especially in this case, because you are so close to the material. There are times when wordiness is a real liability. You can't underestimate the skill of advertising copywriters who churn out thirty- and sixty-second radio or TV spots. And you really shouldn't underestimate the people who create movie trailers. Writing short takes some effort, but you must strive for brevity in this summary.

Start by writing a summary of your screenplay in, say, one or two pages. Then cut all the nonessentials. Pare it down to explaining the arc of the primary story and the character arc of your protagonist. You can include your supporting cast as they interact with the main character.

Conversely, if your problem isn't giving too many details, try this approach: Write the logline. Add to it. Fill in the major plot turns at the end of act one and act two and the climax. Include information about the most important subplot. Build the paragraph from the bare bones of the story.

Once you are down or up to the requested length, read your summary over a few times and see if it makes sense, reveals the flow of the story accurately, and fully clarifies the question raised and how it's resolved. Then set it aside.

Let a day or two go by before going back to it and reading it again. Tweak and correct as needed. But you aren't done yet. You must make this material sound fascinating and unique. You have to make the reader or producer want to read the next sentence. A dull recitation of your plot won't get you anywhere. This seemingly inconsequential paragraph or two has to be the best writing and the best salesmanship you have ever done. It absolutely has to sing.

The Treatment

Some producers, depending on the time they have or the level of their interest, will also ask you for a treatment. Sometimes a request for a treatment comes after you've had a pitch meeting or after they've read the two-paragraph summary.

Treatments are a quick way to cover material for story executives, producers, and agents, all of whom spend a great deal of time reading.

This treatment isn't the one you put together as a guide to writing the screenplay. This is a slicked-up recounting of the final draft of your script, free of notes to yourself, possible other scenes to be included, and all the flotsam and jetsam of the first prewriting material.

So what is this treatment? This material is something between a summary and a short-story version of your screenplay. Like a summary, a treatment briefly retells the story. But like a short story, it must read well; it must make us want to read the next sentence and the next page, and on to the end. The purpose of the treatment isn't simply to rehash the story major beat by major beat and bore everyone to death. And the purpose isn't simply to sell the story idea. It's both.

Your treatment must include:

1. The material that's included in the setup in act one. You need to set the location, era, mood, and tone of the story.

2. The story arc of the main plot, including the turning points. This doesn't mean listing them. This means that you tell it as if you were telling someone a story.

3. Tell this story by focusing on the actions and arc of your main character. That is, a story is about someone who has something he has to or is forced to do. Wrapping the main character and the main plot line together should be automatic, so make sure it is. Your protagonist drives the story by his particular reactions to events, and by making things happen because of his actions.

4. *Very* briefly characterize your protagonist. What kind of person is your protagonist? What's his or her background, approximate age, general look, social standing, and so on?

5. You can include a major subplot, focusing on how it intertwines with and affect the primary plot if it does. It should.

6. It is usually suggested that you include a couple of lines of dialogue so the analyst can get an idea of how you handle the important task of dialogue writing. These lines must be prepared for by the preceding description so that they come in the proper order in the story.

Also, these lines had better be your absolute best in the entire script, and also perhaps the most important—i.e., the plot should hinge on these words. The chosen dialogue should be full of tension and/or wit and/or meaning. Don't put throwaway or bridge dialogue here. None of your dialogue should be flat and banal, but your sample dialogue in the treatment must be your best.

So much for what to include in a treatment. You should also keep the following in mind when you're putting one together:

1. Is the flow of the story easy to follow? Is the hero's goal, need, quest, desire apparent and clear?

2. Will the reader know, without a doubt, which character is the protagonist, i.e., whose story is this?

3. Is it obvious what kind of film is being summarized? If it's a comedy, it needs to read as one; if it's a noir, it must follow the conventions of noir.

4. Is your writing stirring? Does it make the story sound fascinating? Charming? Oddly strange? Searingly honest? This is a sales piece, and it must make the story intrigue the reader.

5. Is the writing strong? Have you used colorful, interesting adjectives? Strong verbs? For example, does your character *take* a drink? Or does he guzzle, swig, sip, nip, quaff, take a drop, swill, gulp, scoff, toss down, knock back, wolf down a drink?

6. Is the writing uncluttered and clean? Is the grammar and usage correct? Has it been proofread? It must be all these things.

7. Does it run between about five and fifteen pages long?

8. Is it double-spaced, are the paragraphs short, and/or is there triple-spacing between paragraphs? You want to keep lots of white space on the page; it makes it look less daunting to read.

No one ever said treatments are easy to write or very enjoyable to read. You need to make yours compelling. And after you have this work done, you are ready to unveil your work to the world at large.

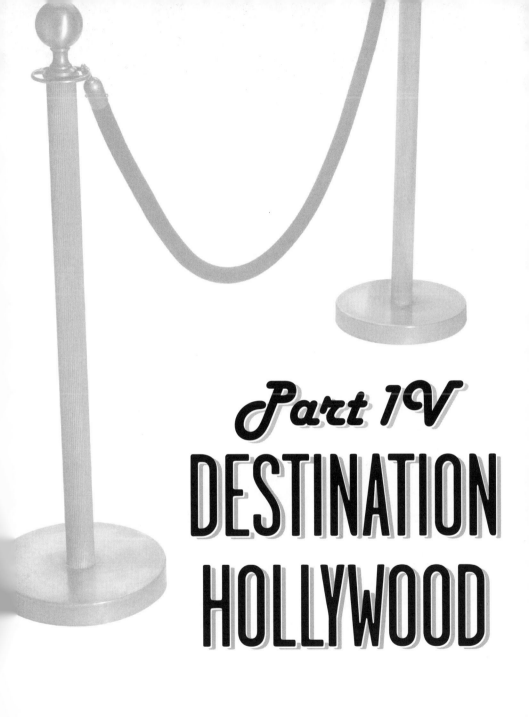

Part IV
DESTINATION HOLLYWOOD

15

The Way It Works in Cinema City

You've come a long way and your journey now takes a major turn. You're finished with the personal part, the part that was between you, Final Draft, and some friends. You've put the finishing touches on the format and overall appearance. You wrote the summary and got the treatment down solid. Now you are going to see if it flies.

There's something important to remember before you loosen the strings on your individually crafted and lovingly designed rig. Headlines can scream of multimillion-dollar script sales or a first-time writer's unbelievable dream deal.

A movie can stir controversy or have cinema buffs heaving in anticipation of its release. A film can feature a top box-office draw and a major studio can release it. But despite any or all of these conditions, the movie can fail and fail miserably. Why? Because whether production executives admit it or not, whether marketing people test-screen the movie or not, whether the studio or company has done everything it can to assure they'll get a good return on their investment, a movie's success is primarily dependent on the script—pure and simple.

"Bankable" stars are important—more for getting the film made than for making a profit—and the value of big-name actors and truly talented ones can sometimes put a marginal film in the plus column. But it's really the script, and don't let anyone convince you differently. Well, okay, there's a caveat here.

Several recent movies, like the comic book–inspired—oops, that's graphic novel–inspired—*Sin City*, showcase such dazzling effects and editing whiz-bangs that people come out of the theater awed. But if pressed, most will say that the story was minimal at best and that all those lead characters sounded like one and the same person since there were no individual voices given to each character. But in the future, when we all get our fill of the amazing things that can be done with the various editing and effects programs, the heart of the matter will remain the story—even if the actors aren't flesh and blood but come from the computer.

A solid budget, a major studio, and big star power didn't help *Beyond the Sea* or *Constantine*, and it most assuredly didn't help *Gigli*. Huge promotional budgets and the appearance of actors on talk shows can enable a film to open big, but even the biggest promotional scheme in the world won't guarantee the film's success. *Troy*, an overproduced, overpromoted film, didn't do nearly as well as expected, and *King Arthur*, another big film, deflated like an unstopped balloon when it was released.

If moviegoers aren't impressed by the story, the theaters will be empty by the second or third week. There are some exceptions. Sometimes it is nostalgia for a classic film that draws people into the theater, like *The Truth about Charlie*. Although it pulled solid numbers at the box office, no one discusses or probably remembers it. When references are made, they're still aimed at *Charade*, the classy original. Sometimes it is an interesting performance or engaging character role that is compelling enough to keep the public lining up at the box office, like, say, John Heder's performance in *Napoleon Dynamite*—an otherwise marginal film whose script displayed no character arc and a forced story arc.

So, as you brave this new journey, remember: The heart of every successful film, the essential engine that runs the show, is the script—that unassuming sheaf of words strung across 110 or 120 pages of plain, white, twenty-pound bond.

As warned earlier, you can't write masterpieces in your garret and expect to be discovered. You've finished your grand opus, but no one will come knocking at your door. Meditation, visualization, voodoo, witchcraft, or offering human sacrifices won't help. Welcome to part two.

This is the difficult half of your quest. You thought the challenging half was taking your idea and forming a coherent story? Nope. Wrong. Now, you've got to get someone beyond your circle of friends and acquaintances to read your script. You have to get your script out there in the marketplace. Take a deep breath. There are ways to reach that destination, and we have the road map.

In reality, writing, like getting a cushy job at a bank, is about being prepared when the opportunity comes along. It's knowing the field as thoroughly as possible. And, given the speed with which business changes, consolidates, and merges, bankers looking for work are forced to be as creative as writers, even if they must direct that creativity into different problems.

We all realize that getting jobs in the "real world" takes the appropriate education, training, preparation, knowledge of the field, and a willingness to keep up with changes. Hopeful writers face the same tasks.

DOING BUSINESS

Before we discuss some of the specific strategies that will help you succeed, there are a couple of things that need repeating about the motion-picture business.

Filmmaking is a business, a commercial enterprise in which companies worry about expenses, overhead, capital investment, planning for the future, and disastrous products. They watch the bottom line very closely—unfortunately, sometimes after the fact.

Studios make movies for many reasons; almost all of them are money. Prestige, winning Academy Awards, and creating or contributing to a company's solid reputation are also reasons studios make movies, but generally they come second. Studios don't struggle for years and years to get an unusual, arty, quirky, profound, or unique movie like *Sideways* made. It is individual writers and producers who do that.

Why, then, are some really awful movies made? And why does a top box-office darling bamboozle a studio into backing a pet project, even if no one likes it but the actor's mother? Because studios think they can make a profit on it.

Additionally, people who work in the movies, like careerists everywhere, are concerned with getting ahead, making the right decisions, looking good to the bosses, gaining notice, obtaining promotions, and getting bigger paychecks. And in the case of Hollywood, many people in the business are starstruck. Not only do they want all the rest, they also want the opportunity to rub elbows with famous actors and be a part of the more glamorous aspects of the field. There is an industry term for these people, but it's not appropriate to use in this book.

It must also be remembered that the people who make decisions about the output of writers, directors, artists, actors, and all the others who comprise film-making crews don't see themselves as part-time teachers helping people become better writers or actors. They expect professional work to cross their desk. They don't have time to see a spark of something in one of your scripts and use their weekends and evenings trying to shape your writing into next year's Academy Award winner just because you're you.

GET TO IT

How do you increase the odds that you will succeed in this highly competitive and exciting field? One of the best things you can do for yourself if you're serious about pursuing your dreams of success in Hollywood is to move to Los Angeles. Don't start reciting all the stuff you hear about "dangerous L.A.," "earthquake-toppled L.A.," or "spread-out, freeway-dependent L.A." Ignore all that stuff. So what if the pollution is bad? How can you trust air you can't see? You know how the media, by just doing its job, inadvertently creates pictures of cities, groups of people, and entities that simply aren't the *whole* story? What you need to know about Los Angeles is that this is where it's happening as far as movies and television are concerned. Every state hopes to lure moviemaking to its turf, and lots of pictures are made outside Los Angeles County. But the business is done here. The scripts are bought here. The planning is done here. And until that changes, here is the place to be.

A bit of common wisdom that floats around Los Angeles contends that you have to stay in Los Angeles until you "make it," then you can move anywhere you want. The assumption is that after your first serious success, or string of small successes, you'll have the contacts you need, you'll have an agent who will work for you, and you'll be able to afford frequent trips to the city to keep abreast of the business. Until that happens, you need to get into the belly of the beast.

Just living in Los Angeles, where movies are a major presence, is preferable to trying to succeed if your address is a village in the Midwest or New England.

Once in L.A., get a job, any job, in the industry. You'll be amazed at what you learn about how things work. You'll meet people who know people. You'll be the first to hear of planned projects, scrapped projects, new contracts signed, and all the rest.

If you don't succeed in landing a job or a job isn't an option or necessity for paying the rent, volunteer your services at the best company you can find that will take you up on the offer. Find out what films are about to start shooting and call around to see if you can work as a production assistant for free. Some film companies take on unpaid interns. Lots of student productions look for volunteer help; call one of the film schools in the area.

Observing firsthand and up close is a strategy that's hard to beat. More specifically, a job on the creative development side of the business that yields information about how scripts are discovered, culled from the piles of submissions, and developed into projects that can be produced is an ideal situation. Working in the legal department can provide solid information about contracts, and accounting can give you a peek at what kinds of deals are cut for the various freelance workers in the business. But working on the creative side or in production is probably the most helpful for your goals as a writer. Here you can see how stories go from the initial pitch meeting to sending a crew to begin shooting.

Barring your ability to actually take up residence in the City of Angels, the next-best thing you can do is find ways to get noticed by people in the business. If you have any connections whatsoever in the industry, ask them for help. If you develop a good rapport, keep in touch with them. Even if you don't develop a good rapport, if you feel their advice can be helpful, keep in touch.

Maybe your aunt works for a producer at one of the studios or the independents. Call her. Maybe your father went to college with a guy who's now working at one of the production companies. Call him. Even if he works for a law firm that handles some entertainment companies, he's bound to know a thing or two about the industry. Maybe you haven't seen an old friend of yours in years and heard at your last high school reunion that she works in the business. Call her. Most people love being asked for their advice, whether or not they eventually take a genuine interest in or help you with your career. Oftentimes people you contact can give you names of other people to talk to, and then you are on your way. Talking to various people will give you some feeling for how the business operates. And remember, it is a business. Better yet, once you've made a good contact, try to get to Los Angeles and visit that person. When it's suggested that they go to Los Angeles, some writers sigh deeply and confess to hating Los Angeles, or hating the traffic. They express concern about the crime or the bigness of the place. What's really happening is usually fear—fear of looking like an idiot, fear of high-speed freeway traffic, fear of getting lost, and fear of the irritation and stress that result from trying to find addresses in an unfamiliar and hugely spread-out city. There's the fear of rejection, of feeling like the smallest tadpole in a very large swamp. There's a hate of Los Angeles just because it's Los Angeles. And, some feel they will become fodder for the entertainment machine and come out an automaton, losing the individuality of vision that's reflected in their screenplays. They really want to stay put and do independent features.

Everyone feels more comfortable in her hometown, where she knows her way around and feels that she has some contacts and control. But if you really want to succeed at this, you've got to go. At the least, you've got to visit, get a feel for the place, and meet whatever contacts you've managed to establish. Those contacts might very well lead to other contacts and other people to talk to.

Even better, if you can swing a six-month sabbatical to the entertainment capital, you should do it. Spending time in the City of Angels helps because it will:

- Give you a chance to see how the industry works

- Give you an L.A. address, at least temporarily

- Provide an opportunity to take advantage of the many programs, classes, presentations, and offerings around town

- Let you get familiar with the town so it won't seem so foreign later if you need to attend meetings

- Provide information about the industry, from the *Los Angeles Times* and *Daily Variety* to overhearing your neighbors argue about which one should audition for George Lucas's or Jim Cameron's next movie

- Get you away from all those people at home who keep you from writing

- Give you the opportunity to meet people in the industry, which may lead to meeting more people in the industry

- Provide the possibility of doing something really stupid that may catch the eye, ear, attention, or curiosity of someone who then might like to meet the nut and subsequently agree to look at your script

- Give you the chance to see if all the horror stories you've heard about L.A. are true or exaggerated—after all, about fourteen million people live in greater Los Angeles, so there must be something attractive about it

- Encourage you to diet. You'll notice as you make your way around the industry and the places where people connect to it that there aren't many fat people . . . okay, that's an exaggeration, but take a look when you get there

- Give you a chance to look at the real estate and pick out the area where you want to live once the script sells—when you see the prices for homes, you'll understand the high cost of making movies

If you aren't convinced you should pack your bags, even for a temporary trip, you can try the following strategies for getting someone to take a look at your work. Even if you do move to the city, you should use these methods as an adjunct to your other efforts.

There are lots and lots and lots of scripts floating around the industry. You have to break through and get yours seen. It takes persistence and toughening up your ego.

The Internet can sometimes work as a substitute for settling in the Big Orange. As mentioned earlier, there are dozens of Web sites focused on screenwriting, and many tout the number of scripts from anywhere and everywhere that have been discovered on their site. There are also dozens of screenwriting competitions. All of these may help (or at least won't hurt), and if things work out well for you, they might eventually lead to at least a trip or two to Los Angeles. You won't arrive as a V.I.P., but you'll at least have an interview with someone.

Another long-distance way to gain some knowledge and background about the business is to keep abreast of the field by subscribing—whether online or hard copy—to one of the two industry trade papers, *Variety* and *The Hollywood Reporter*. You'll want to take advantage of these resources. What you want to get from your reading and research is an understanding of the industry. Generally, think of yourself as applying for a job at the bank. You know that you must prepare yourself for a job at the bank. Does work in Hollywood deserve less? You know it doesn't. This *is* your career choice. This *is* your life, right? Enough said.

16

The Big Sell

Before you go any farther, you've got to take one more step so the world will know who crafted your high-flying script. Register your screenplay with the Writers Guild. There are two ways to do this: online or by mail.

Online, you will complete the form and submit it before you send (or e-mail) the entire script with the cover sheet you'll print from their site (*www.wga.org*). For regular mail, create a cover sheet that lists the title of the material and your full legal name, social security number, address, and phone number. Attach this sheet to an unbound copy of the script, enclose a check for $20 (for nonmembers), and send it to:

WGA Registration
7000 West Third Street
Los Angeles, CA 90048

THERE'S MORE

The Writers Guild also publishes a list of agents—hard copy and online. For a small sum it will send or e-mail you the list. Get one of these as part of your selling campaign. You can also go online and see what else it has to offer. It won't be wasted time.

In addition to this list, there are several other directories of directors, writers, agents, production companies, and more. The best known of these is probably the *Hollywood Creative Directory*, which lists hundreds of companies doing business in Los Angeles, including the television networks and cable outlets. The information includes executives' names, the company address, and the types of films they make. Get these lists and directories. Mark those companies that have produced movies in the same genre and for the same medium as yours.

IT'S WHO YOU KNOW

There are various ways to try to sell your material. One way is to get an agent to represent you. The best method of getting an agent is to know one or to have a friend who is represented by one. The friend recommends you, and the agent is almost automatically more interested in you than he is in the huge pile of scripts he has stacked next to his desk. The big agencies—ICM, CAA, etc.—won't even let you send a script to them unless you're recommended by one of their clients. You've got to try to find someone who can recommend you—a friend, a neighbor, a friend of your mother's, or any other relative with whom you're currently on speaking terms. This person doesn't even have to be a friend. He could be an acquaintance or someone you meet at a party or a coffee shop. If the person is a writer who's got an agent, ask if you can call the agent. It's worth a try. Remember, Hollywood is a town where chutzpah is admired.

If none of this works for you, use the Writers Guild list you purchased. This short directory will note which agencies are willing to look at new writers and which are not. Call all the appropriate agencies. Ask them if they employ an agent who handles unproduced or unrepresented writers, and define what kind of writer—television or feature—you are. Some agencies specialize in sitcom writers or television-drama writers. The large agencies have both types on staff. If an agency has a staff person who represents new writers, she probably will tell you to send a query letter outlining your story and briefly detailing your experience as a writer. The smaller agencies, which may have as few as one agent, will tell you whether they are looking for any new clients. If you speak convincingly about your project, they may relent and invite you to send a summary.

CALLING

You want these phone calls to go as smoothly as is possible. The most important thing to remember is that your pitch should be delivered with enthusiasm for your project. The feeling among agents and production companies is that if you're not a believer in your work and in yourself, why should they believe in you? After introducing yourself, mention that you think their company or agency might be interested in your material—it's their kind of project. Follow that with a brief two-liner about the material, summing it up in its best, sexiest, hippest, most intriguing wrapping. Add a couple of lines about yourself—your experience as a writer and why you're a writer they can believe is serious about succeeding.

If this is the first thing you've ever written and you don't have any professional writing experience, mention the classes and training you've had. If you get a chance, you might mention your intimate connection with the topic of your screenplay (if you have one), which may make up for your lack of writing experience. Remind yourself that John Grisham was an attorney, not a creative-writing teacher, before he wrote his first book.

Once your phone script is honed, there's another step to take. Like a corporate public relations person preparing the company president for a public appearance, you should make a Q & A, a list of remarks or questions that you might get from the assistant or agent. Prepare answers to them. The answers should convey that this material is worthy of the company's consideration and you as a writer are worthy of the name.

Get your names, your phone script, and your Q & A, and start warming up your dialing finger. Try to forget what your telephone bill will look like at the end of the month.

TALK IS CHEAP

When you call a production company you might not get a chance to go through the whole script and you'll have to improvise. There are fairly standard responses to inquiries. The assistant may tell you:

- Send a synopsis

- The company isn't looking for material at the present time

- They don't accept any material not represented by an agent

The assistant wants to get you off the phone as fast as possible.

If the assistant puts you through to the creative affairs person or a development person, chances are, that person will tell you the same things the assistant did. But, you've succeeded at this step and you deserve a pat on the back for it.

If you're lucky enough to get through to one of the story people, he will probably be even less interested in having his time wasted, but more interested in an intriguing story. In that oh-so-brief moment that you have that story person on the line, sell your heart out. Every development person is looking for the next great film—if his company can afford to make it and if he thinks it can make money. One hard-working writer recently used this call-around approach and got two companies to agree to look at his material. One of them, HBO, even returned the message he left.

If you are calling an agent, she may tell you:

- The agency only takes writers referred to it by writers it currently represents

- The agency isn't taking on any new clients at the present time

- Send a synopsis and someone will get back to you

If you convince the agent to let you send a synopsis, make sure you know what length she wants. Make sure you get the person's name, spelled correctly, whom you should send the material to. When you write the synopsis, make it the best writing you've ever done in your life. Remember, as was detailed earlier, this summary is half story summary, half sales pitch.

If the assistant tells you to have your agent send the material, he may just be trying to get rid of you; he assumes you don't have an agent. And you don't. But if you feel strongly that your story is right for this particular company, be persistent. Volunteer to send it with a release form. Ask the assistant what he suggests you do. Your enthusiasm, confidence, and belief will help you overcome some resistance.

One thing you should remember about these phone calls: Institutions that receive thousands of inquiries sometimes behave as if they possess treasure that everyone wants. Since their phones are constantly ringing, they get weary and impatient, and it's obvious in their voices when they speak to you. It's a learned behavior.

There are also receptionists and phone operators who are so impressed that they share the same physical space with the entertainment VIPs who pass by their desks that they figure you are nothing but a meaningless mite in the universe. Then there are the clerks who have failed to learn anything about the company they work for and consequently haven't any idea to whom you should speak.

Most of the larger agencies are businesslike, and because they're answering inquiries like yours so often, they give you the minimum amount of time possible. So, don't be surprised that making these phone calls isn't fun. Don't take them personally. Write down your goal for each phone call, and don't let yourself stray from it because of some rude, illiterate Gen Xer whose development was arrested at age twelve.

When you're invited, whether it's by an agent or an agent's assistant, to send a script, make sure that you have the agent's correct name and spelling and all other necessary information—department name, if it's applicable, the agency name with the correct spelling, the address, etc. It's a good idea to learn the name of the agent's assistant. You probably will be talking only to her throughout your contact with that agent. If you can make phone friends with her, so much the better. As a former assistant to a head of production at a studio once said, "Writers don't know how much I can help or hinder their dealings with my boss. If they did, the arrogant ones who call would be a little friendlier." There is another saying in Hollywood: "Be kind to assistants. Next year, they may be sitting in their boss's seat." Always keep these two bits of advice in your mind when making your calls.

There is one more piece of information you ought to know about agents' assistants: Since so many people want to work in the industry, there are plenty of talented people to choose from. Agents' assistants, who almost without exception want to become agents, in some cases already have a law degree. Most assistants have at least a BA tucked into their portfolio. So it's probably not smart to talk to them as you might occasionally talk to the burger flipper who can't make change for a dollar.

MAIL IS CHEAPER

Another way to tackle getting agents or production companies to take a look at your work is to write them a query letter that contains the same material as your phone script. Leave lots of white space on the page. Put the one-paragraph synopsis on a separate page. Make sure your name is on it and that it is attached to the letter. Send the material to a specific person. Just call the company and ask to whom the material should be directed. Again, get the correct spelling of the contact name.

When you query companies or agencies, you're not asking permission to send the logline and summary, you're just sending it. The downside of using the mail is that letters tend to be easy to overlook and get lost in that large stack of incoming scripts.

E-MAIL MAY WORK

A third alternative is to send your inquiry by e-mail. A couple of writers I worked with were successful in getting the opportunity to submit their material through this channel. However, with the proliferation of electronic mail, there's a good chance it may be deleted without so much as a peek at its contents.

But every avenue, promising and not so promising, should be used, and it doesn't take much time to go online and seek out studios and companies. As with the other methods, get the correct spelling of the correct person's name at the company you wish to approach, then e-mail that person directly, if possible. And don't be too familiar just because it's e-mail.

Another strategy is to go online and find out where and when a pitch session will be held. There are annual pitch workshops sponsored by magazines and writers' groups. Get yourself to L.A. to attend one or more.

FOLLOWING UP

Follow up on all agencies that invite you to send a script or a query letter. Make a list of the companies you've called, and note the ones you've subsequently contacted by mail. Keep a chart. After a couple of weeks, call those agencies you've sent a script to. If you're not interested in keeping track of your script, no one else will be either.

If your script has been read when you call after two weeks, that's a plus. You'll get your answer and can move on to the next step. Usually, however, nothing will have happened to your work. But your call will serve as a reminder to the agent or as an impetus for her to read the script. During this call, you'll want to remind the agent of the script's content and genre. If she hasn't read the work yet, ask her when you might call again. And then call at the time suggested by her— or a little sooner.

Agencies range from very organized and straightforward to those that don't seem to have a clue what it is they're doing. With the latter type, you wonder how they make any money. Example: A writer I know sent two scripts to a small agency that she thought had only a single agent. The agent sent the feature script back with a note that she liked the writing, but wasn't too crazy about the story. She had passed the television script along to the agent in the office who handled TV. He would be getting back to her. Two weeks later, the writer called the TV agent. He didn't seem to have any idea what the writer was talking about, so she started from the beginning, describing the path her script had taken. The television agent then said, "Oh, yes, here it is. Give me a week to read it." She did. A week later, she called again. He again didn't have any memory of their conversation or her script, but promised to "look for it." Two weeks later, it was much the same story. The writer gave up, figuring she didn't want to be represented by an agent this disorganized, forgetful, or possibly deceitful.

The ideal scenario is that the agent likes your script, tells you he'll represent it, and asks you to sign an agency contract. That means the agent will represent those scripts you write that he feels are worthy/salable for the term of the contract. It means he's serious about you, and he'll probably do some work for you. He sees promise in your writing. This kind of arrangement is rare for new writers.

The second-best thing that can happen is that an agent will like the project you've sent her and agree to represent it for a specified period of time. It is more likely that an agent will tell you verbally that she likes your script, and then get very vague about it. She won't mention a contract.

When you actually talk to an agent who's interested in your writing, it's almost guaranteed that she'll ask you what else you've written (although you've sent her a brief résumé of your writing) and what you're currently working on. Don't ever admit that you're not writing anything. The agent needs to be convinced that you're a working professional writer who's in this for the long haul.

Once an agent is interested in what you've written and agrees to represent you, you can't relax. Some agents are serious and hardworking—they don't take on clients casually, and they work for them—but don't count on it every time. It really depends on the agent. Many agree to send your work out to some producers, but whether they do or not, you don't know. Some say they'll represent you and don't do much of anything except go to lunch and schmooze.

You don't want an agent who has dedicated his professional life to lunch and whom you suspect can't read. But in the beginning, you probably should take whatever you can get—it's usually only temporary.

If an agent agrees to rep your script, you should keep tabs on what the agent is doing or not doing for you. Discuss with him what his strategies are for marketing your work. He's supposed to be the inside person, with up-to-date information on which companies are doing what. Your agent probably won't know everyone—that's hardly possible—but he should be abreast of current developments, trends, and productions. Let him know you're willing to do what you can to help the process along.

You also should learn as fast and as thoroughly as you can which production companies might be looking for a script like yours or which companies produce work that is similar to yours (e.g., an action script should be sent to those companies that make action films). You can learn this by reading the trades, by purchasing (on paper or online) the latest issue of a studio directory, by talking to the people you know, and by noting what companies and producers have made the movies currently screening at the neighborhood theater. When you find companies that you think might be interested in the type of material you've written, ask your agent if he has considered sending your script to that company. Don't let it stop there. If you feel your material would be right for a particular company, but after talking to your agent you realize he doesn't seem familiar with the company, call the company yourself, tell the executives there about your project, and ask them if you can have your agent send them the project. If they say "yes," call your agent and tell him that the company's expecting it. Make sure you give your agent all the appropriate information for their cover letter and subsequent calls. Ask the agent to fax you a copy of the cover letter he writes to the production company.

You don't want to become passive as soon as an agent agrees to represent you. You can't depend on agents to do all the work for you. There are ambitious agents who will read your stuff, sign you on, and immediately work for you day in and day out—along with their other clients—but it's better if you don't count on that. Instead, continue working for yourself.

MAKERS OF MOVIES

Another way to get your script into circulation is to solicit independent producers. Again, try to get in contact with these people through friends and acquaintances, or through anyone you meet or work with who may know a producer.

Producers who have well-established companies and contracts with studios, like Ron Howard and Jim Cameron, will insist that your script come in through an agent.

But there are producers all over the place who are looking for solid projects they can develop. Some have agreements with studios or networks and continually make movies. Some are well established, have a good track record, and have good relationships with studios or networks. Other producers have been involved in a couple of films, have some contacts, and are always looking for the screenplay that will make them rich and respected.

Finding independent producers isn't too hard. Most are listed in the directories and are mentioned in the trades when new deals are completed. The good thing is that some independent producers will read your material without insisting that it come from an agent. When you contact these producers by phone, letter, or e-mail, you should follow the same approach as you follow when contacting agents.

Producers, like agents, have varying degrees of ability to get films made, and various levels of professionalism and influence. You can, therefore, expect a variety of responses when sending them material. Some will agree to read your script but never get around to it, while others will read it promptly and contact you with their response. Producers have three primary concerns: finding material they want to produce, getting a distribution deal set, and finding financing for the production. Often small producers, who are usually only involved in one production at a time, will be unable to look at your work or unable to get back to you about it in any reasonable amount of time if they're in the middle of a production.

There is one notion you need to get out of your head regarding producers: You won't be submitting your precious, refined, and erudite work to some overweight, gold-chain-wearing, cigar-smoking ape who can't read. That's not to say to say there aren't some marginal characters wandering around calling themselves producers. Yes, there are producers in Hollywood who don't know one end of a camera from another, but most of these guys don't last long. For all the laughs this stereotype engenders, that guy probably disappeared when his gold chains turned green.

BEING LESS DIRECT

There are a couple of less-direct ways of getting your work out of the nest to see if it can fly on its own.

One route you can take to get your material out in circulation is the screenplay contests that seem to abound; most are listed on the Net. Entering these competitions is easy. Winners are usually promised a cash prize, from $250 on up. Included in many contests is an introduction to a Hollywood agent. There is more information about contests in chapter 22.

There are some that are high profile enough that the winners and runners-up are briefly "hot." It can last for a couple of months, give or take. If you're a winner, it's important that during this time you run as hard and as fast as you can to make contacts and get your script placed with a company that will actually produce it.

If nothing much comes from winning the award, you can still use your prize as leverage. When calling agents, mentioning that you've won a script competition will probably make the agent more amenable to reading your work.

Film festivals focus on finished films, but some include a writing competition as well. It's probably a good idea to check them out.

THE RISKY ROUTE

There is another method of getting your scripts in front of someone's eyes. Well, it's not one way. This avenue is really lots of ways, depending on your creativity. If you don't shrink from risky games and can bluff your way through tough situations, the Shameless Stratagem method may be the technique for you. In this approach, your creativity is your salvation or your damnation.

Pose as a messenger boy and deliver your script to a top agent. Get the home address of an important producer or actor, dress as a pizza delivery man, and deliver your script instead of a large one with anchovies. Frequent the places where producers and agents hang out, and buttonhole whomever you think is appropriate. Send an agent a series of notes touting your screenplay. Treat your screenplay like a Saturday serial and send a little at a time to a producer.

Use your imagination and come up with your own ideas. If the conventional routes don't appeal to you or don't work out, you can try the Stratagem. But keep in mind that this approach isn't for the faint of heart or faint of pride. You may be embarrassed. You may be ignored or treated as if you are crazy. You may be brushed off like lint on a lapel. But there's always the chance that you may intrigue someone and get him to look seriously at your script. And if it works out, you've already got a good start on acquiring an interesting reputation, a plus for anyone on the creative side of this business.

17

Helping Yourself

If Charles Dickens were around, he might apply the opening thoughts of *A Tale of Two Cities* to Hollywood, for Movieland is both tacky and refined, is home of the worst and best movies, and is both cruel and nurturing to artists of various specialties. It is the primary place where you experience rejection from agents, producers, studios, and various employers. It is also the place where you can find nourishment and comfort. It is here that you find others who share your interest and your plight. It is the best place to gain knowledge, advance in your craft, and suffer periods of enforced leisure.

After a day spent beating on doors, trying to get one to open to you, there are things you can do that may help you along your way.

IT'S ALL IN THE SCRIPT

One way to increase your writing confidence is to know what professional scripts— scripts that have been produced—look like, how they read, and what kinds of stories they tell.

If you live in the Los Angeles area and want to browse through scripts without actually laying down any hard cash for them, the Academy of Motion Picture Arts and Sciences (*www.oscars.org*), the Writers Guild, and the American Film Institute (AFI; *www.afi.com*) provide libraries that include film and television scripts. Their libraries are open to the public. Call or visit their Web sites to get their hours of operation.

If you're willing to spring for copies of your own, the better to study and mark up, there are stores in the Los Angeles area that sell them in their real form; that is, on regular bond, bound with brads.

Book City

Book City (*www.hollywoodbookcity.com*) is a mail-order store that sells scripts for $15 unless they exceed 150 pages; then, the charge is $20. You can order by phone (323-466-2525) with a Visa, MasterCard, or American Express card or you can go online. The mailing cost is $5 for the first screenplay, with $2.50 added for each additional script ordered.

Hollywood Collectables

Hollywood Collectables is another mail-order house that will sell you a script in its raw form. They charge $15 for television scripts and $20 for features. Buy four scripts and the fifth one is free, or buy eight or ten and you get two or three free, respectively. That price includes shipping and handling. You can call them for a catalog.

Hollywood Collectables
120 South San Fernando Boulevard, #446
Burbank, CA 91502
Tel. (818) 845-5450

Downloading Screenplays

If you're up for reading scripts on your computer screen, there are several sites that offer downloadable screenplays. Keep in mind that these sites generally have lots of advertising and offer other products. Sometimes it takes several links before you even see a screenplay. The following can get you to a screenplay: *www.script-o-rama.com*, *www.simplyscripts.com*, and *www.scriptpimp.com*. Sometimes it almost seems as if getting scripts on the Web is more trouble than simply ordering by mail.

BOOKS HELP TOO

Old-fashioned but nonetheless very current and user-friendly, bookstores offer lots of products to aid the writer.

Larry Edmunds Bookshop

For the past sixty-five years, Larry Edmunds Bookshop (*www.larryedmunds.com*) independent has specialized in volumes about entertainment. The store has just about any book you need in the field, and if it doesn't, the staff can get it for you. They also can order a script, if that's what you need. There are some exceptions, and you've got a better chance of getting the screenplay if it's contemporary, but they can fill most orders. You can find them at:

> Larry Edmunds Bookshop
> 6644 Hollywood Boulevard
> Hollywood, CA 90028
> Tel. (323) 463-3273

Samuel French Bookstore

Samuel French Bookstore (*www.samuelfrench.com*), which began in New York City, caters to theater professionals. It continues to carry copies of plays and related theatrical books, but it also stocks all the pertinent film books that writers need.

> Samuel French Bookstore
> 7623 West Sunset Boulevard
> Los Angeles, CA 90046
> Tel. (323) 876-0570

> 11963 Ventura Boulevard
> Studio City, CA 91604
> Tel. (818) 762-0535

The Writers Store

The Writers Store (*www.thewritersstore.com*) was founded as a hardware and software store with "some" books. The owners changed their location and dropped the hardware lines they carried. Now they specialize in computer programs, books, and other materials writers need.

The Writers Store
2040 Westwood Boulevard.
Los Angeles, CA 90025
Tel. (800) 272-8927

Book Soup

Although this isn't a specialty store for writers, Book Soup (*www.booksoup.com*) offers quite an array of books and materials, and it is in the heart of Hollywood. You can find it at:

Book Soup
8818 Sunset Boulevard
Los Angeles, CA 90069
Tel. (310) 659-3110

Opamp Technical Books

Opamp Technical Books (*www.opamp.com*) is just what it says it is. Although it doesn't carry many books on screenwriting, it carries technical books on film-making that you might find helpful or interesting.

Opamp Technical Books
1033 North Sycamore Avenue
Los Angeles, CA 90038
Tel. (323) 464-4322

Quixote Studio Store

Quixote Studio Store (*www.quixotestudios.com*) is a hybrid store that's worth mentioning. Among other film-related products, it sells some books, but more importantly, it carries the stationery materials that writers need, like script covers, paper, brads that are the right size and weight, software, contracts, and all the rest. Interestingly, it is also about the only place around where you can still find production boards for scheduling shoots, which are still preferred by some unit production managers and assistant directors, despite the availability of computer programs that have replaced them.

Quixote Studio Store
1021 Lillian Way

Hollywood, CA 90038
Tel. (323) 876-3530

Of course, Borders and Barnes & Noble are on the Net. You probably already know this, but just in case you've forgotten, go to *www.amazon.com* (they teamed with Borders online) and *www.barnesandnoble.com*. What they don't offer is the bookstore experience, a chance encounter, a change of mind at the last minute and the spontaneous pause for reflection that can occur upon reading an interesting passage.

MAGAZINE AND TRADE PAPERS

There are magazines and newsletters that offer some comfort, information, and aids for your pursuit of writing work. Keep in mind that you shouldn't read too many success stories in these magazines. Just read enough to spur you toward your goal (and maybe your own interview one day), but at the first sign of feeling overwhelmed, when you sense your confidence is draining away, stop.

Most of these magazines offer writing tips, industry news, often an interview with a writer who has recently sold material, sometimes an article by a script consultant or analyst or similar insider, and other miscellaneous information.

Written By

Written By magazine is a product of the Writers Guild and is probably the most stable and established of the screenwriters' magazines. This journal regularly features a couple of interviews with writers, either newly emerged or well established; discusses Guild topics; features short articles on writers' issues, problems, and experiences; and covers miscellaneous topics of interest to screenwriters. If you believe in the idea that one way you can get closer to your goal is to visualize yourself being a successful writer, then having lots of information about the Guild will encourage more realistic scenarios.

Written By
Writers Guild of America (WGA)
7000 West Third Street
Los Angeles, CA 90048
Tel. (323) 782-4522
E-mail: *writtenby@wga.org*

Creative Screenwriting

Creative Screenwriting (*www.creativescreenwriting.com*), a journal published six times a year, considers itself a magazine for the professional screenwriter, not the wannabe screenwriter. It features articles on writing and focuses on the development of scripts to make them salable. On the back pages, it occasionally runs a listing of spec script sales. You can get a subscription for $29.95, or you can pick up a copy at Borders, Barnes & Noble, Waldenbooks, and various independent bookstores.

Creative Screenwriting
6404 Hollywood Boulevard, #415
Los Angeles, CA 90028
Tel. (800) SCRN-WRT or (323) 957-1405

scr(i)pt

In *scr(i)pt* (*www.scriptmag.com*), a bimonthly magazine, the focus is on the craft and the business of screenwriting. You will find articles similar to those in other screenwriting magazines. It goes for $29.95 for a year's subscription. Otherwise, you can usually find copies at Borders, Barnes & Noble, and other upscale outlets.

scr(i)pt
5638 Sweet Air Road
Baldwin, MD 21013
Tel. (410) 592-3466

Fade In

Fade In (*www.fadeinonline.com*), which originally focused on writing, has broadened its coverage and now also covers the ins and outs of the business and industry buzz. The cost of a year's subscription to this quarterly is $19.95; two years is $26. It sponsors its own screenwriting contest and highlights upcoming competitions. It sponsors the Power PitchFest, held annually.

Fade In
289 S. Robertson Boulevard, #465
Beverly Hills, CA 90211
Tel. (800) 646-3896 or (310) 275-0287

Hollywood Scriptwriter

For over fifteen years, screenwriters have had yet another source of information and shared wisdom. Billing itself as the trade paper for screenwriters, *Hollywood Scriptwriter* (*www.hollywoodscriptwiter.com*) features interviews on the craft and business of the industry, as well as interviews with writers. A subscription will cost you $35 in the United States and Canada, $50 for all other countries.

Hollywood Scriptwriter
P.O. Box 11163
Carson, CA 90746
Tel. (310) 530-0000 or (866) HSWRITER

P.O. Box 10277
Burbank, CA 91510
Tel. (818) 845-5525

Scriptwriters Network Newsletter

The Scriptwriters Network (*www.scriptwritersnetwork.org*) publishes a monthly newsletter that covers what's going on in the industry, membership news, and a couple of regular columns, including a summary of the group's monthly meeting and speaker. To get the $40-per-year subscription, contact:

Scriptwriters Network Newsletter
11684 Ventura Boulevard, #508
Studio City, CA 91604
Tel. (323) 848-9477

Film Quarterly

Published by the University of California at Berkeley, *Film Quarterly* (*www.film-quarterly.org*) journal includes discussions and critiques of recent films. So, if you would like to take a break from structure, characterization, and plotting, you can pick up this journal and see what their writers have to say about the symbolism, the artistic merit, or the political, psychological, or philosophical implications of certain films.

Film Quarterly
Press Journals
University of California
2120 Berkeley Way #5812
Berkeley, CA 94720-5812
Tel. (510) 643-7154

Daily Variety and The Hollywood Reporter

More important than general magazines for finding useful material that may directly aid your quest are the two trade journals, *Daily Variety* (*www.variety.com*)

and *The Hollywood Reporter* (*www.hollywoodreporter.com*). Both cover the business five days a week. It is in these news outlets that you can find out who just sold a big script; if a new agency is forming; which agents have, in *Variety*'s terms, "ankled" their present agency for a new one; which studio chiefs have left and who has taken over for them; and much more about the daily world of the industry.

They also write about new companies that have formed and usually include information regarding the type and number of films the new companies hope to produce. Both publications also run box-office and television ratings reports, gossip columns, and want ads.

Daily Variety
5700 Wilshire Boulevard
Los Angeles, CA 90036
Tel. (323) 857-6600
Annual subscription: $299

The Hollywood Reporter
5055 Wilshire Boulevard
Los Angeles, CA 90036
Tel. (323) 525-2150
Annual subscription: $229

DIRECTORIES

Though they don't feature page-turning prose, directories can supply helpful information about the industry. If you want to know where to contact an agent or a director, for example, you can find him in the appropriate directory. Look for directories such as *Writer's Guide to Hollywood Producers, Directors, and Screenwriter's Agents* and *Annual Agency Guide* in Samuel French or Larry Edmunds. You can also search for members of the Directors Guild of America using the online search engine at *www.dga.org*.

Special mention must be made of the *Hollywood Creative Directory* (*www. hollyvision.com*). Called the "phone book of Hollywood," it offers listings of all the production companies, from the major studios to one-man operations, doing business in Los Angeles. It lists all the pertinent script personnel at a company; their phone numbers; and whether they do commercials, television productions, or features. Often included are the titles of some of the movies and/or television shows the companies have completed. The directory is published three times a year. Recently the company has added directories of distributors, agents, managers, and others. You can order directly or subscribe to the online version.

> *Hollywood Creative Directory*
> 5055 Wilshire Blvd.
> Los Angeles, CA 90036
> Tel. (323) 525-2369 or (800) 815-0503
> E-mail: *hcd@hollyvision.com*

WRITING GROUPS

Writing is an isolated and isolating occupation, and after years of spending so much time with only a word processor for company, many writers' social skills are rusty. That's only one reason why writers' groups can be good for a screenwriter. There are other reasons as well. Some groups allow you to present your work and give you critiques. Some hold annual writing competitions and seminars with people in the industry and host monthly speakers and workshops. And writing groups enable you to get to know others who do what you do.

Despite the natural competition among you, groups are more often than not a positive experience. Sharing writers' problems can diminish their significance. And you may meet people who know people who know people. By encouraging others in their careers, you'll wind up with a lot of contacts when they all, you included, move to the next step.

Writers' groups can be found listed on bulletin boards at the better bookstores. Sometimes there are listings in the book section of the Sunday newspaper (or whenever your local newspaper runs its book news and reviews). Attending lectures by visiting writers or Hollywood teachers can also provide opportunities to discover people who belong to writing groups. Bookstores feature appearances by writers with newly released books. Mixing with this crowd might turn up people involved in writers' organizations. The local library is also a place to look for possible groups to join. Writing classes are another place to find groups.

Writers Network

Writers Network (*www.fadeinonline.com*) group offers a script library, script coverage and analysis, and occasionally free advice. It also holds an annual screenwriting competition and its PitchFest, at which you get the opportunity to pitch your project to over a hundred agents and producers. The group publishes an agency guide that covers only literary agents with notes indicating what kinds of material the agents are looking for.

Writers Network
289 S. Robinson Boulevard, #456
Beverly Hills, CA 90211
Tel. (800) 646-3896 or (310) 275-0287

Scriptwriters Network

Scriptwriters Network (*www.scriptwritersnetwork.org*) is an all-volunteer organization for writers. It holds a general meeting the second Saturday of each month, to which industry speakers are invited. It also offers a producers outreach program for connecting writers with producers. It does staged readings, holds scriptwriting competitions, and offers various other advantages for struggling, mostly non-produced writers. Membership is $60 per year and includes a subscription to the newsletter, detailed earlier in this chapter.

Scriptwriters Network
11684 Ventura Boulevard, #508
Studio City, CA 91604
Tel. (213) 848-9477

BACK TO THE BASICS

If you don't feel your skills are at a sufficiently professional level yet, or if you fall into that category of people who are always looking to improve on what they've got, or if you're just looking for a warm room where you can share your writing woes with others in a similar situation, you can check out writing classes.

Most colleges, universities, and community colleges offer at least one screenwriting class—usually more, since the great American screenplay has replaced the great American novel as the goal of many writers.

If you really want to sink your teeth into studying film and get into first-rate writing classes, there are three standard schools that most everyone in the business considers the holy three. As Yale and Harvard are to law, these schools are to film studies. You can contact them for program specifics. Two of them offer graduate degrees with a specialty in writing.

University of California at Los Angeles (UCLA)

The University of California at Los Angeles is a large state university in west Los Angeles that offers undergraduate degrees in film and television and an MFA in screenwriting (*www.tft.ucla.edu*). Competition is very tough. The graduate writing program is small and highly respected. It funnels lots of writers into successful careers and provides lots of personal interaction with faculty and other writers.

> University of California at Los Angeles (UCLA)
> School of Theater, Film and Television
> 405 Hilgard Avenue
> Los Angeles, CA 90024
> Tel. (310) 825-5761 (film studies)

University of Southern California (USC)

The University of Southern California (*www-cntv.usc.edu*), or SC, as the natives refer to it, is a private institution in downtown Los Angeles that offers a BA in film and television production, a BFA in film writing, and an MFA in screenwriting.

> University of Southern California
> School of Cinema-Television
> 3450 Watt Way
> University Park, CA 90089
> Tel. (213) 743-2736

New York University

On the opposite side of the country lies the third school. New York University (*www.tisch.nyu.edu*) is a private four-year school, located in the heart of New York City and offers BFA degrees in film, television, radio, and video. There is no specific screenwriting major. An MFA in film is also offered.

> New York University
> Tisch School of the Arts
> 721 Broadway
> New York, NY 10003
> Tel. (212) 998-1700 (undergraduate film)
> Tel. (212) 998-1780 (graduate film)

Other prominent and highly regarded schools that offer specialties in screenwriting include:

American Film Institute

The American Film Institute (*www.afionline.org*) is yet another school with an excellent reputation. Their Center for Advanced Film and Television Studies offers a program in screenwriting. Completing the one-year program can earn you a certificate of attendance, but if you already have a BA degree, you can earn a master's at the completion of the two-year program. Students without undergraduate degrees do not receive college credit for courses taken here. As with the other leading schools, the competition is stiff.

> American Film Institute
> Center for Advanced Film and Television Studies
> 2021 North Western Avenue
> Los Angeles, CA 90027
> Tel. (323) 856-7628

Chapman University

Chapman University (*www.ftv.chapman.edu*), an up-and-coming private Southern California school, is in the process of expanding its film school after receiving a large grant. The curriculum includes a screenwriting specialization.

> Lawrence and Kristina Dodge College of Film and Media Arts
> Chapman University
> One University
> Orange, CA 92866
> Tel. (714) 997-6815

The advantage of attending the preceding schools isn't simply the instruction, the opportunity to study with other bright, talented students, and the possibility of rubbing elbows with people actually working in the industry. There are also lots of special events, presentations, and extracurricular film-related activities that you can participate in and take advantage of.

Of the four-year schools, there are several that offer degrees in, an emphasis in, or special programs in screenwriting.

Columbia College of Chicago

Columbia College of Chicago (*www.colum.edu*) is a relatively small private school that boasts a rather large film department. Students who choose screenwriting complete a core of lower-division classes that includes a couple of writing courses. The last two years focus on advanced screenwriting and writing-related classes.

Columbia College of Chicago
600 South Michigan Avenue
Chicago, IL 60605-1996
Tel. (312) 663-1600

Columbia University

Columbia University (*www.columbia.edu*) has one of the oldest and most distinguished film programs in the country. The graduate writing focus is a three- to five-year program that includes various writing classes, revision classes, and workshops. The completion of two feature scripts is required, one of which serves as a thesis project.

Columbia University
2960 Broadway
New York, NY 10027-6902
Tel. (212) 854-2815

Loyola Marymount University

At Loyola Marymount University, screenwriting is one of five areas of emphasis students can choose. The undergraduate program requires fifteen lower-division writing classes and upper-division classes that include writing, editing, adaptation, and directing. The school encourages its students to take classes outside the writing field.

Loyola Marymount University
7900 Loyola Boulevard
Los Angeles, CA 90045
Tel. (310) 338-3033

School of Visual Arts

School of Visual Arts (*www.schoolofvisualarts.edu*) offers a four-year program in which students can choose to concentrate on screenwriting beginning in their third year. Studies include screenwriting clinics, the business of screenwriting, and other writing-related classes. A feature-length work written with a mentor is the final requirement.

School of Visual Arts
209 East Twenty-Third Street
New York, NY 10010
Tel. (212) 679-7350

There are a couple of community colleges that offer programs in motion-picture production and offer multiple levels of screenwriting classes:

Scottsdale Community College
Motion Picture and Television Program
9200 East Chaparral Road
Scottsdale, AZ 85254
Tel. (602) 623-6000
www.sc.maricopa.edu

Los Angeles City College
855 North Vermont Avenue
Los Angeles, CA 90029
Tel. (323) 953-4000
www.lacitycollege.edu

Beyond these institutions, there are dozens of schools around the country that offer degrees in film; film and video production; film, radio, and television; or some combination of these. Most of these schools don't emphasize screenwriting. Their curricula are divided equally between studies in film production and studies in film history, theory, and aesthetics.

Other Classrooms

If you already have a degree and aren't looking for a complete program, or if you're looking for individual classes in writing, you should check out the universities or colleges, including community colleges, close to you.

If college classes don't appeal to you or require more commitment and cash than you can muster, there are always the short-term writing classes that are held around Los Angeles and around the country by people recognized by the industry. These teachers offer short-term workshops, held on weekends or over four or five weeks. Some emphasize a particular approach. If you can't take their classes, you can find their books, and in some cases, audiotapes.

Syd Field
270 North Canon Drive, #1355
Beverly Hills, CA 90210
Tel. (310) 271-1839
www.sydfield.com

Robert McKee
Two Arts, Inc.

12021 Wilshire Boulevard, #868
Los Angeles, CA 90025
Tel. (310) 312-1002
www.mckeestory.com

John Truby
Truby Writers Studio
751 Hartzell Street
Los Angeles, CA 90272
Tel. (800) 33-TRUBY or (310) 573-9630
www.truby.com

The New York Film Academy has branches in New York City, London, and Los Angeles. They offer one-week to two-year sessions on filmmaking and acting. There is also a one-year screenwriting program.

New York Film Academy
Universal Studios
100 Universal Plaza, #9128, Suite 179
Universal City, CA 91608
818.733.2600
www.nyfa.com

Writers Boot Camp has been around for some time, getting students to go from idea to finished script in six weeks. You can find them at:

Writers Boot Camp
L.A Headquarters
Bergamot Station Arts Center
2525 Michigan Avenue, Building 1
Santa Monica, CA 90404
(800) 800-1733
www.writersbootcamp.com

And if none of the foregoing is quite what you're after, there are dozens of screenwriting workshops that range in length from one to five days. Two of the more prominent of these are the Screenwriting Expo, held in Los Angeles each Fall and the Screenwriting Conference in Santa Fe, held each June in Santa Fe, New Mexico.

18

Maybe You've Got Other Ideas

There is more to scriptwriting than the big screen. One prominent television writer began as a mystery writer and moved to television. He said that being a writer-producer of a television show was about the best that it got in Hollywood. He could write a script for the hour-long detective show and it would be produced and aired in under a month. Further, as a staff writer-producer, he was a part of the entire process. According to him, to write material, be a part of the production team putting it together, and see it aired on national TV a week or two later was the penultimate position to be in.

In feature films there are many situations in which a script, purchased or optioned, falls off track. The writer is thrown back to square one. In features, it can be years between the day the first word is committed to paper and the day the screen is ablaze with the story. If a screenplay survives all the vicissitudes of the development process, it will be, at the very least, upward of two years before the prints are shipped to theaters around the country.

CONSIDER OTHER VENUES

Many writers, in their quest for big-screen success, forget that there are many places where they could employ their ability to tell stories. The world doesn't end with feature films.

In terms of money and renown, writing television movies, hour-long series, or sit-coms is the next best thing to features—and it's getting more equal all the time. Everyone knows, or sort of knows, the names Don Bellisario and Dick Wolfe. Do you know or do you remember who wrote *Spider-man 2* or *Legally Blonde*? In TV, often-times the money is better, more consistent, and more regular. Although television production companies always try to wring the cheapest contract out of every writer hired for staffs of sitcoms or hour-long shows, the money is still good.

COMEDY CAN BE KING

There's a lot of pleasure and prestige in being a successful comedy writer. You don't need any ambitions beyond this to sleep well at night. The really good ones are not a common commodity in Hollywood, and experience in this area is highly valued. It's accepted in Hollywood that there are only a handful of individuals in town capable of running a network. There are only a couple of handfuls of people the networks turn to develop new sitcoms, and there are only a half-dozen handfuls of successful, proven comedy writers. It's the big leagues.

Television comedy writers face a difficult working situation that can be a killer for the inexperienced or the uncertain. Writers must develop twenty-six minutes of comedy; include at least a couple of story lines; make it funny; make it fresh; write it so it fits the personalities of continuing characters; write it under time constraints; accept criticism from the executive producer, the network, the actors, and just about everyone else associated with the show; take notes after the first read; rewrite; do more rewrites during rehearsals; and so on until the cameras start rolling.

If you are a writer who firmly believes that one of the important elements of writing is to express your personal views—philosophical, political, sociological, or otherwise—that, too, can be achieved in sitcoms. There's little doubt about where writers stand on various issues when you watch a half-hour comedy series. And you don't even have to build an episode around a specific theme like, say, illegal immigration. A minor character can voice your opinion, as long as you weave it into dialogue that's witty and works with the story. Imagine having a national audience for your opinions on abortion or the Presidency or Social Security. Imagine seeing your name on the credits of the show each week. Imagine a cushy paycheck every couple of weeks. And imagine working with a staff of people who are as bright, funny, quick witted, and ambitious as you. That's scary. And that's meant in a good way.

Finally, writers on sitcoms can aspire to positions that carry more responsibility and prestige. Most producers of successful sitcoms began as writers and eventually formed their own companies. And if you get into a position where you *create* a successful show, then you're a god—a creative god who also takes big checks to the bank every time an episode or rerun of an episode is aired, even if you only wrote a few shows during the sitcom's three-year-plus run.

How do you get into this work? Are you funny? No, I mean *really* funny? Do you think funny? Can you write? Following is a super-express course on sitcom writing.

Stories for half-hour sitcoms are different from features. They're written in a two-act structure. Act one, comprising the first fifteen minutes of the half hour, is basically the setup for all the story lines. There are generally at least two story lines (called the A and B stories), although some series, like *Scrubs*, often have a story for each of the major characters. In act one the writer has to set up all these stories and get the coming complications in place and foreshadowed. In act two the complications develop and eventually everything goes wrong, or if not wrong, differently from what was intended. The finishing touch is the post-climax result of the misfired schemes.

Writers have to keep in mind that the characters they are writing for are already established. You can't write things that would be out of character for any of the sitcom's personalities just to make your joke or your entire script work. You can't create new characters or give one of the show's ongoing characters a different back story than has already been established. You are limited to creating minor one-episode characters when writing a spec script.

You really have to rack your brain for an idea the staff hasn't already done. Sure as you tell them you have a story about how the characters get stuck at a dairy farm, the story editor will reply that they did that plot line two years back. You had better watch the shows you want to write for—so you'll know before you write what stories have already been developed and produced.

By watching the sitcom for which you want to write, you'll also determine the established setting used on the show. Some sitcoms are quite confined, and you'd better place your story in those sets. Others, like *Sex and the City*, are very liberal with the movement of characters. But remember, most of your scenes will have to take place in maybe three different locations for the entire half-hour. Most of *Two and a Half Men* takes place in the home of the Charlie Sheen's character. Most of the *Friends* episodes took place at the two groups' apartments and the coffee bar where they hung out. Don't try to create new locations for your spec script. Every addition costs money that the business affairs people will insist isn't available.

The format for sitcom scripts is different from the format used with feature films. You need to know what that format is before you submit your spec scripts. It will be taken as a sign of amateurism if your work is not completed properly. Formatting TV series scripts is detailed in chapter 12.

Breaking into television is as difficult as breaking into features. Maybe harder. The best thing to do is write spec scripts. Keep writing them. Look for an agent who specializes in television writers. If agents turn you down, keep trying until you get one. You have to keep writing new scripts for current shows. Having sample scripts for *My Three Sons* or *Family Matters* probably won't impress an agent or a sitcom producer.

Television sitcoms strive to be very cutting edge. Styles, attitudes, and approaches change quite rapidly in this area of television writing. You have to stay on top of them to succeed.

DRAMAS WORK TOO

Hour-long shows occupy a place midpoint between sitcoms and feature work. When you think of it, an hour-long show is really half a feature film.

The similarities to sitcoms include continuing characters, established sets, and a consistent routine or format. On *Law & Order*, the first thirty minutes are consumed with arresting the person or people whom the detectives have determined committed the crime that opened the show. The last half is devoted to the prosecuting attorneys and their efforts to make a case. As a spec writer, you won't want to mess with this format, just as you won't mess with *ER*, *Desperate Housewives*, *Monk*, or any other established hour-long show.

You need to understand the unique approach taken to the established characters on the show that you wish to write for. *Law & Order* spends very little time on the personal lives of its characters. Things are hinted at, asked about, and referred to, but very little is seen on screen of the characters' personal lives. It's very much the same for all of Dick Wolfe's shows. They are about the process of or raise questions about the law. You need to keep the style of the show you want to write for in mind.

On *Monk*, the situation is nearly the opposite. The show is equal parts a seemingly impossible-to-solve crime and Monk's peculiarities, phobias, and ongoing grief over his wife's death. His personal life has an important effect on his crime-solving and on his interactions with his sidekick-nurse-aide.

One of the differences between sitcoms and hour-longs is the locations. Hour-longs, shot like film, use many different locations in addition to their established or "home" sets, e.g., the White House on *The West Wing* or the CTU (Counter Terrorism Unit) Center on *24*.

Hour-longs are written in four acts, each running about fifteen minutes. The story arc is very much like that of feature films, with acts two and three substituting for act two of a feature. Many sixty-minute scripts also include a prologue or a teaser of one and a half to two pages in length. It is aired before the opening commercials to get you involved. The format used for hour-longs is the same as features, with the exception that the acts are labeled.

Many series will not accept spec scripts written for their shows. As a reading sample, it will be suggested that you submit scripts you've written for shows other than the one you're approaching. You can see why producers might be wary. If they ever produce an episode similar to yours, they could be vulnerable to a lawsuit. If the show you've written for refuses to see spec scripts of its show, you should submit a script for a similar show. If *Law & Order: Criminal Intent* wants to see a sample of your writing, but not a *Law & Order: Criminal Intent* script, send them a *CSI* script or a script for another *Law & Order* show.

You can find out which shows are buying and the person at the company to contact if you subscribe to *Written By*, the Writers Guild magazine. There are listings of current television shows in that publication. Checking the show's Web site can also often provide you with the necessary information for submissions.

MORE VEINS OF WRITING ORE

Commercial, established network television is very competitive, offers good pay, and can be very satisfying writing (whether you admit it or not). Cable networks now have their own established series—many of which have won critical praise and awards. Generally, in cable, the pay is not as generous. The competition is also fierce, but there may be a few more doors that can be pried opened. Cable is less restrictive and generally more liberal with what is aired, whether it is violence, sex, or obscenities. Cable also has a reputation for being more experimental and open to fresh ideas regarding the types of shows, topics, length, timing of a season, and practically everything else. The downside is that they usually have less production money.

If you have experience writing news, you can always investigate the possibilities of writing for one of the many newsmagazines on TV. These programs also have staff writers and producers, and they buy freelance pieces. Their material is, naturally, very topical and often slanted toward what they consider investigative, but they also buy lifestyle pieces.

This isn't narrative writing. It is more closely allied with print journalism. Experience at a local television station or a newspaper, as well as an undergraduate degree in broadcasting or journalism, helps your chances of entering this area.

Reality shows, which are finally waning somewhat, range from the "thinking man's" *The Amazing Race* to various short-lived, artificially enhanced "reality" shows like *The Will*. The producer-writers on these shows don't spend much time at their word processors.

If you have experience writing other types of nonfiction material, there are shows on the Biography Channel that may offer you some possibilities, as will the History Channel, the Discovery Channel, and the Learning Channel. The material they present is much like magazine-feature writing.

There is another kind of writing that can be very lucrative and delivers a large audience. Some call it a form of fiction and in many, many cases, the material is wonderfully bright, witty, cutting edge, high-budget, and well crafted. It tells a story in the briefest of seconds. It's advertising; yes, advertising. The reason we watch the Super Bowl. If you write one of the spots seen on that broadcast, you've hit the peak of your copywriting career. Don't underestimate this form of the craft of writing. Yes, you're writing in order to sell something, and that sounds like groveling with the lowest of the low, but people who can tell us a whole story in thirty or sixty seconds can't be disregarded. It's a real skill, and there is an art to doing it well.

Some of the stories, of course, aren't fresh or interesting. Since TV first flickered in our living rooms, we've seen dozens of versions of the same material, such as tales of harried women looking for just the right cleaning product or someone burdened by heartburn. But other advertising spots are clever, fresh, and memorable. Many times the expensive productions appearing in high-priced time slots don't tell us a story at all. Like poetry or photography, they simply evoke a mood, share an emotion, provide a fantasy, stimulate a daydream, or suggest a sense of belonging to something. To accomplish this effort, a high degree of skill is required. And for all you know, like someone who prefers poetry to novel writing, you may be better at writing thirty-second spots than full-length features.

Writing television commercials will require a background in advertising copywriting, and usually experience in ad agency work. It is also a highly competitive field, and well paid when you get out of the back room and into an office with a window.

You have little or no opportunity to weave in any personal ideas or philosophies. And, besides your boss and fellow staff members critiquing your work, there's the almighty client. They have the final say in anything you create, regardless of whether the Clio committee has already praised early drafts of your campaign. And one failed advertising campaign can buy you a ticket to Palookaville.

Nonetheless, writing television advertising material has similarities to feature-film and television writing. Many of the same skills are required. As an advertising writer, you are much more restricted with regard to the usual narrative elements, but much less restricted to a linear, narrative structure. Your fantasies can take many forms.

As a copywriter, though, you are a flack for business and industry. You aren't communicating something important to your audience or trying to make them laugh or telling them a fascinating story, you're trying to convince them to spend money, buy a product. The ethics of that is something you have to work out. The work itself is very creative.

If you really want to write scripts, why restrict yourself to feature films? There are areas like industrial film, training videos, and educational productions that can be fulfilling, creative, and well paid. So, while you're nursing that screenplay each night from twelve to two, you might consider one of the other areas from nine to five.

19

Yes, It's the Agent Question Again

Agents are like bank loans. You can get one if you don't need one, and if you need one, you can't get one.

Getting an agent takes persistence, having written something to show them, and a willingness to be treated with less respect than a death-row prisoner. But don't be too hard on agents. Well, you can be a little hard, but give them just the tiniest of breaks. They have a lot of people banging on their doors. Those supplicants think the agents can do something for them. If agents have people soliciting their attention all day long, eventually they may begin to feel that they possess some kind of magic. Maybe they get smug and start treating people with the same dignity they usually save for cockroaches. Contrariwise, maybe they just get weary—weary of bad writers, writers who don't learn the business, and writers who think they are the Second (or First, if you're Jewish) Coming. Then again, maybe they just need time to do the work that is on their desks before moving on to the next phone call or plea from an unknown.

It may seem like agents mostly go to lunch and schmooze, but they are probably working. A lot of their work *is* schmoozing. Successful agents work for their clients, so they don't have much time for untried writers. If you were a current client, would you want your agent wasting time with an unknown instead of negotiating a better deal for you? No, probably not.

Agents know how hard it is to sell the work of new writers. It's a double sell: the script and the script's author. And if the script isn't a high-concept work or doesn't have an easily identifiable audience, then the agent has to work doubly hard. The representative has to convince someone at the studios that the script would make a successful movie, despite the fact that it isn't based on a video game or comic book, isn't a coming-of-age piece, and doesn't feature characters under twenty-five.

As a beginner, how do you deal with this? Besides following all the previous suggestions in this book, you ought to know something about the agencies. Start calling agencies. Ignore most of the advice you get about who does and who doesn't look at new writers' work, and call them. If you can get a bit of your pitch out to someone at the other end and he responds even semi-favorably, you've just got your toe in the door—ever so slightly. Later the toe may get slammed on and hurt like hell for a day or so, but it may also be the mini-break you've been looking for.

If you really don't have any contacts in the business, you have to be ready for some hard knocks, and playing the percentages is probably better than picking out a couple of agencies and investing your hopes and schemes in them. Better to spread your efforts around at the beginning. Even if you don't have any success, you've got a bit more experience with the telephone script you've written for yourself and you're getting smoother and smoother at it. To give yourself comic relief, replay the "Gotta Dance" scene from *Singin' in the Rain*.

THE AGENCIES

Agencies range from one-person offices to huge conglomerates that represent writers as well as actors, directors, and sometimes other clients like large corporations. These places are so potent that they tell the studios what movies to make.

That's an exaggeration, but not much of one. As you might have guessed, there is an agency hierarchy, from the most prominent and prestigious on down.

There's every chance that the largest and most prestigious agency won't take the time to talk to an unrepresented, never-represented, unproduced writer. If you want to skip them in your search, it will be easier on your ego, but you should know who they are.

If you consider yourself a working writer or an aspiring writer, then you must know **Creative Artists Agency** (CAA - *www.caa.com*). This is one of the agencies that has so much clout that you genuflect when you pass the building.

Creative Artists Agency (CAA)
9830 Wilshire Boulevard
Beverly Hills, CA 90212
Tel. (310) 288-4545

ICM is another acronym you should know. It is short for International Creative Management (*www.icmtalent.com*), which has been around since the early 1970s and has had its good days and bad days. Usually it's fighting with CAA to be considered number one in the hearts (for those who have hearts, that is) of industry people.

International Creative Management (ICM)
8942 Wilshire Boulevard
Beverly Hills, CA 90211
Tel. (310) 550-4000

Then there's the classic **William Morris Agency** (*www.wma.com*). Founded at the turn of the twentieth century, this is the most historic and is the only one that's earned a place in the language as a generic reference to agencies.

William Morris Agency (WMA)
151 El Camino Drive
Beverly Hills, CA 90212
Tel. (310) 274-7451

Other agencies that aren't quite as firmly rooted in the Hollywood firmament, but are equally able to make deals, include:

Endeavor
9601 Wilshire Boulevard, Third Floor
Beverly Hills, CA 90210
Tel. (310) 248-2000

United Talent Agency (UTA)
9560 Wilshire Boulevard, #500
Beverly Hills, CA 90212
Tel. (310) 273-6700
www.utaproductions.com

Broder-Webb-Chervin-Silbermann Agency
9242 Beverly Boulevard, #200
Beverly Hills, CA 90210
Tel. (310) 281-3400

The Gersh Agency
232 North Canon Drive
Beverly Hills, CA 90210
Tel. (310) 274-6611

Paradigm
360 North Crescent Boulevard
North Building
Beverly Hills, CA 90210
Tel. (310) 288-8000

Writers & Artists
924 Westwood Boulevard, #900
Los Angeles, CA 90023
Tel. (323) 866-0900

The following are also good at what they do and may be a good place to start:

Agency for the Performing Arts (APA)
9200 Sunset Boulevard, #900
Los Angeles, CA 90069
Tel. (310) 273-0744

The Artists Agency
1180 South Beverly Drive, #400
Los Angeles, CA 90035
Tel. (310) 277-7779

Innovative Artists
1505 Tenth Street
Santa Monica, CA 90401
Tel. (310) 656-0400

Shapiro-Lictman-Stein
8827 Beverly Boulevard
Los Angeles, CA 90048
Tel. (310) 859-8877

You will probably be all right with any of the above if you can get them to look at your material, but don't consider this list an endorsement of them or a condemnation of those not included.

BOUTIQUES

Your third choice is to go for a boutique agency. These smaller houses are probably your best bet. It's hard to know, without visiting them personally, how businesslike, how busy, and how reputable they may be. Outside of pretending to be a flower delivery person with the wrong address, it's difficult to simply walk into an agency to take a look around, although you might give it a try.

A more economic approach to cull the wheat from the chaff is to ask around about smaller agencies. Such agencies generally specialize in one medium or the other. If you take writing classes or attend workshops, other attendees can be valuable sources of information about agents. This kind of gossip can be good. If you have neighbors who work in the business, ask them what they know about agencies.

If you speak with someone at an agency that isn't taking clients—and you're more likely to have an actual conversation with someone at a small agency—ask him if he knows of any agencies that are open to new clients or if he knows of any new agencies that are being formed.

A newly formed organization might be the best thing for you. New agencies are hungry to succeed, and their client roster probably isn't yet full—unless the principals came from other agencies and brought every single one of their former clients with them.

Reading the trades can help you with your search. When a new agency forms, it is covered by the journals. When a deal is made, the agent involved is mentioned in the article. Other tidbits can be found throughout the various features that are run each day.

During this fight to be noticed by an agent, it's nice to get some perspective on the problem by remembering that you are hiring someone to do something for you. When you hire a painter or a plumber, you look for the best deal for the least money, and you choose. But when it comes to agents, even though they are the vendors, so to speak, you don't get to pick and choose. In your current position, you look for agents, but agents get to choose who they want to rep.

There's no guarantee that you'll be treated better or worse by large, midsize, or small agencies. There is a mixture of rudeness and kindness at all levels. A super-small agent may be more willing to listen, but it may be because he has nothing better to do. One thing that is admired in the business is persistence, and when it's perceived, others, including agents, are often willing to help because they admire the drive and are familiar with the struggle for recognition.

There is another alternative. If you're willing to do the calling, you can get an attorney to represent you. He won't sell your material or schmooze over three-hour lunches, and he may or may not have contacts, but studios and production companies can accept material sent to them by attorneys. If this tactic appeals to you, it's best if you hire an entertainment lawyer who's familiar with writers' contracts.

20

Once Inside, What Happens?

Getting your script inside the doors of an agency, a production company, or a studio is a pivotal step in your quest. It is here that your script will get its first, and maybe only, consideration and ultimate judgment at that company. That consideration and judgment comes, in almost every case, from a script analyst. These people are the ones who analyze your screenplay from cover to cover. This may be the only time your work gets read and thought about at the company you've sent it to. Many times, the analyst will determine the future of your work, or whether it has a future at that company.

It's probably a good idea to examine the route your script takes and the people along the way who will be considering, evaluating, and ultimately judging your material. It doesn't matter whether a screenplay or teleplay is submitted by a heavy hitter from a top agency or forced through the door by a struggling writer; you can be pretty sure that every script in Hollywood—the big deal and the small— that becomes a major motion picture playing in a theater near you follows this same route.

Depending on how small the company is, agencies and production companies receive anywhere from a couple of scripts to dozens each day. The studios and major production companies receive maybe a hundred or so a week. The flow of scripts varies so much that it is difficult to put a hard-and-fast number on it.

After the mail is opened or the delivery person has made his drop, the scripts are logged in. This is done so the studio, production company, or agency can track them. Sometimes executives and producers are waiting for a script that they're expecting from an agent. It may also be that other companies are alerted to the script and there may be bidding on it. Or an agent may have opened bidding on a project by contacting all the major production companies simultaneously. If any of these is the case, the script is given the rush treatment. The executives/ producers will probably read the script concurrently with the analyst. Everyone, in this case, works against a time restraint, and all the necessary forces are pulled together to determine and plan the company's action. This is almost the only time executives get in on the reading of scripts this early in the game.

At the next level, a script may not be generating as much heat as the scenario described above, but nonetheless, the work is from an established writer, or maybe it's part of an agency package that includes a production company or an actor and/or writer and/or director. This material is also often considered rush, although the executives may not read the material until after the reader finishes and reports his or her impressions.

The next step down in this process is the regard accorded to material that is the work of a well-established professional writer with good credits, but whose current project isn't set up with any production company and doesn't have any prominent actors or directors attached. The story editor assigns the script to be read immediately or overnight.

More commonly, scripts come in from an agent without any fanfare or attachments. These scripts will be treated routinely. The story editor checks them in and puts them on a stack of scripts to be read. Analysts pick up the scripts, read them, and write their reports without undo hurry.

In the case of agencies, it's slightly different. At a large agency, where a new writer has to be recommended by an existing client, the material comes to the agent and is sent to the story editor to be assigned to an analyst. At agencies that have a staff member assigned to review new writers, material—received at the invitation of the agent—will come into that person's office. If the agency uses readers, the material will be given to one of them for review. If the agency is small, the agent or the agent's assistant will probably read the material. This also holds true for small production companies, although at some production companies based on studio lots, the material is covered by the story analysts working for the studio. Different studios and different production companies handle it the way they think is the most efficient.

At the very small or one-person agencies or production companies, it pretty much depends on the person who runs the business. If you've convinced them on the phone to take a look at your work, they may do so immediately—or they may never get around to it. You should probably start calling them after two or three weeks. That way, they'll know you're interested, like a good salesman, and you're not just a passive cog to be ignored forever. Your script probably won't have been read when you call, although there are exceptions.

Scripts submitted to various-sized agencies and productions companies often are read promptly, but then the coverage (the reader's analysis of the work), especially if the reader recommends that the executive take a look at the script, sits on that executive's desk for some time. You should call back in a couple more weeks to keep tracking it. If you continue to get vague answers and no one can even tell you whether it's been read, well, you have to decide how long you want to pursue it before considering it a dead issue with that particular company.

The process here can stretch on for weeks and weeks, although the coverage may have been assigned and completed within the first two. Executives, like the rest of us, have twenty-four hours in a day, but reading coverage or even a script often become a low priority as they shepherd their current projects; answering the long list of telephone calls from agents, people looking for work, the crew of the current projects, and industry contacts; and keeping up with ongoing developments in the industry that might generate future projects or offer sources of financing. In the larger companies, after positive coverage comes in, executives often read the material on the weekend. Producers and story executives are famous for toting home bags of scripts for their "weekend reads."

There are times when producers are already sold on a project—probably a project they've had a hand in developing somewhere along the line—and ask a reader to do an analysis so they can get another point of view. In these cases, even if the analyst doesn't find promise in the script, the producer will probably go ahead with it. But the reader's input has been sought so that the producer will have another perspective on the material's assets and failings.

THE ANALYSIS

As with every other aspect of the business, analysts come in all varieties. There are no particular credentials required. At small agencies or production companies, the agent or producer may read your material. Or they may have their latest assistant read it, and she could be anything from a Paris Hilton to a PhD. But more often, your material will be read by people who make a living as script analysts, have been doing it awhile, and consider themselves professionals.

Since script analysts can wield life-or-death power over your work, at least at the company they work for, you ought to know something about them.

Analysts, or readers, are part of a nearly invisible force in Hollywood. They don't usually enjoy power lunches with big-time producers or stars, they don't call their agents daily, and their pay doesn't rate headlines. Mostly readers sit in silent offices working through a stack of scripts and turning in their reports. Or in the case of freelancers—the majority of analysts—they sit at home in an easy chair or at a desk or in bed at any time of day or night, reading through a stack of scripts, writing their evaluations, and hauling them into the office the next day. Every month, thousands of scripts get churned through the business in just this manner. The process isn't glamorous, financial scandals don't arise here, the process doesn't get covered by E!, and few people outside the business know how it works.

As with every other area of the entertainment industry, there is a union to cover these workers. In this case it is the Readers Guild. Any company that is a signatory to the International Alliance of Theatrical Stage Employees (IATSE) contracts must employ only union readers. This includes the major studios. The union assures members an equitable pay scale and first chance at openings at signatory companies. Readers must work for a signatory company for a period of thirty days before they can apply for membership in the Guild. I'm sure you see the catch-22 here.

Experienced professional readers fill the Guild's roster. People who get into the Guild are freelance readers with lots of experience. As explained earlier, there is lots of talent to choose from in the business, so lots of educated, well-qualified people fill all sorts of jobs. Most analysts have earned at least a bachelor's degree; many have graduate degrees too. The fields of study are varied, but the majority hold degrees in English, film, or theater.

Although the industry is too often accused of being a "boys' game," in the area of script analysis, the field is pretty evenly divided between men and women. The age of analysts also runs the gamut, from people in their early twenties, still studying at UCLA or USC film schools, to experienced hands who've been with one company or another for twenty years or more.

A majority of the readers employed in Hollywood aren't in the union. For the most part, they too are experienced professionals who make their living reading scripts. Some readers choose not to be in the Guild, some see no advantage for their particular career goals, and some haven't yet had the chance to join.

Readers are a pretty diverse lot. Some make this a career, some are published or produced writers and hope to pursue goals in that area, and some see the job as a rung up the ladder on the creative side of the business. From the position of analyst they may hope to become a story editor, creative director, or production or story executive, and maybe eventually a vice president of production. Few script analysts consider reading a permanent career, but there are those who find fulfillment in it and plan to stay.

Despite their various career objectives and general diversity, script analysts are pretty much in agreement when it comes to their work. Not surprisingly, the most common trait shared by those surveyed is their love of movies, especially good movies, and their love of the process called Hollywood. They want to see lots more good movies during their lifetimes; hence, they're always looking for good scripts.

Another characteristic all analysts share is a love of reading. That's probably why they've gravitated to this job. They have always been good readers and have always enjoyed it. It's second nature to them. Like children, readers want to be told a good story, with characters that come alive. Analysts hope every script is a page-turner. Unlike the ordinary reader, the script analyst must be able to imagine the story on the screen.

UNHAPPILY, IT'S TRUE

Readers, whose daily lives are filled with reading scripts, find that writers make the same mistakes over and over. The most common errors they stumble upon that persuade them the script isn't worth their company's investment usually involve the story's characters and the events detailed in the plot.

In weak screenplays, the characters are very predictable people and the events of the story have been done in dozens or hundreds of films. In short, the whole thing becomes a cliché. Essentially, the analyst knows what's going to happen in the story after reading three or four pages. Analysts really don't need to read any more, but they're paid to and sometimes they're hopeful that things will swing around to something interesting. It creates a situation in which readers have to force themselves to turn the pages rather than looking forward to the surprises yet to come.

Too, too many screenplays have no original voice, topic, or indication that the writer has firsthand knowledge of anything other than writing. The screenplays written by these authors describe movie reality, not real-world reality, and the story feels borrowed from the movies. Worse, when the writer focuses on, say, a police intervention, a major league baseball team's operation, or events in a business office, it's painfully obvious that the writer hasn't done any research and has no experience with any of these areas. The ignorance is revealed in each scene that's written, and consequently the material doesn't feel true.

Sometimes writers get so wrapped up in trying to work through the plot that they ignore their characters. Creating a one-dimensional character may work for films based on video games and some simple, Schwarzenegger/Seagal/Van Damme action film, but everything else needs living, breathing characters with some individuality.

The analyst is tempted to wonder whether the writer ever actually talks to people, observes them, or tries to get under their skin. The characters on the page don't suggest an interior life. Equally off-putting are characters analysts find impossible to care about. If there is nothing in the protagonist that draws us to him or her and nothing to make the character worth rooting for, then the analyst isn't invested in the hero's journey. Protagonists must be passionate. Even if they're wrongheaded and want something for the wrong reasons, they have to care so that we care about them.

Although readers may get bored, they stick with a screenplay to the end, turning each page, hoping to find originality, something that will spark interest, a creative approach to the plot development or the hero's problem.

After the reading is complete, the analysis is put to paper. The reader first notes the pertinent information about the script: the title, the writer, the agency representing it, the genre, the time period, the length, and so on. There's some variation among studios, but not a lot.

Individual elements of the script get box scores. The items that are rated normally include: premise, story line, characterization, structure, and dialogue.

They are usually rated: excellent, good, fair, or poor, although some companies have a code that is known only to the readers and executives. This is an attempt to keep the intentions of the studio from leaking to other companies. At the bottom of the rating scale is the crucial item: Does the reader recommend a "pass"—that is, a rejection? Or does the reader recommend acceptance of the script? Or does the reader recommend a "maybe?" An acceptance or a maybe usually gets the script a second read. At some companies, readers can write an addendum to explain their reasons for recommending the script. Some studios give analysts four choices: pass, not recommend, consider, and recommend. These categories or some variation of them are used by companies that employ analysts.

Readers follow their box scores with a synopsis of the story. As you've already guessed, the reader writes something akin to a book report. Different studios have different requirements here also. Some like them very long, two pages double-spaced or maybe single-spaced, while others prefer four or five paragraphs on any story they get.

The final and most crucial portion of the task is the analyst's critical comments. It is here that the analyst will discuss what he or she sees as the essential strengths and weaknesses of the material's premise, story line, characterization, plot, structure, and dialogue. Some readers include their estimation of the commercial possibilities of the work.

With the great numbers of scripts they read, analysts estimate anywhere from 5 to 30 percent can be characterized as "good," with some analysts estimating that about 40 percent of what they read is "competent" work. Readers often despair that some very good scripts will never get made because they don't reflect current trends or because they're not highly commercial.

If the reader recommends that the company pass on the project, i.e., turn it down, the analysis, along with the script, is returned to the producer who brought the project in or to the story executive who accepted the material from an agent. The producer reads the coverage and, in most cases, accepts the reader's recommendation and returns the script to the agent or writer. There are times when the producer may find something of interest in the coverage of a screenplay that's been rejected by the analyst. If the producer retains any interest in a project after reading coverage that recommends a pass, or if the work is the product of a writer the producer admires or has obligations to, he or she might assign another analyst to the project. If this happens, the script gets a second chance at impressing a reader. This second read usually confirms the first reader's recommendation, and the script is ultimately rejected.

If agencies turn down your project, they'll return the script to you (some smaller agencies require that you send them a self-addressed stamped envelope) with their rejection letter. They don't include the coverage.

If your script is returned, your task is to pick yourself up, dust yourself off, and start all over again by getting back on the phone. We've all heard the stories of writers submitting their work to dozens and dozens of producers before anyone expressed any interest.

When an analyst gives your material the green light, your screenplay and its coverage follow a different path. At a studio or large production company, the material and the coverage will be returned to the producer. After reading the coverage, she will decide whether she wants to pursue the project any further.

Although the producer may agree that the material's good, she may not personally respond to it enough to pursue it. She may like the writing and will consider you for other writing assignments she may secure. She may like the idea, i.e., the premise, but remain unimpressed by the writing. In these cases, the producer will pass, buy the idea and give you story credit, and hire other writers to rewrite it. Or, she may like the material enough to try to develop it. Producers can also offer to option the material for a set period of time, or they may arrange to buy it.

If someone in the company loves the material so much that he or she is willing to fight for it, this is a good thing. Scripts that have an advocate inside the company stand a much better chance of being produced. It may result in a production deal for the writer. Or, after a few battles, the executive fighting for your script may weary of the fight and let the project drop.

One way or another, your work has to impress the script analysts who will be reading it. Remember, readers are not your enemies. They can be your advocates at the company. If they really like a piece, they write about it positively, and they too can champion it as the process proceeds.

Studios and production companies can only produce a very small percentage of the scripts they receive, but analysts want to like what you've written. They like finding good material. They want something wonderful to read. They always hope that the next script is going to knock their socks off. When you pick up a novel, you want to get immersed in it. Readers also want to dive deep into your script and not come up until the final page. And if, during the course of their read, they learn something new about a profession, an event, about history, a geographical area, or a group of people, so much the better.

Readers want to find good scripts they can enjoy, care about, remember, and promote. They keep looking for them. Let's make sure your script is the one they love, the one they want to see play out on the big screen.

21

Options Outside Hollywood's Turf

If your attempts to get an agent or production company to look at your material meet with no success, consider yourself one of the family. It happens to thousands of writers.

Being turned down can signal a dozen different things. It can mean that the agency doesn't represent the kind of work you sent it. It can mean the agency has no good contacts with the television show you wrote a spec episode for. It can mean the agent isn't taking on new clients. It can mean the agent just lost his assistant and doesn't have time to read anything, and it can mean that the month your script came into the agency, the agent was ill or traveling and simply had to skip whatever stacked up during that time.

As you already know, and have heard over and over (and that's just in this book), this is a very competitive business. There are so many scripts out there that they are like notes in bottles, bobbing about a crowded sea, searching for someone to pick them up. Agents can't read them all, producers can't read them all, no one can read them all.

Every agent, producer, and studio in town wants to find the next big film—the film that will win an Academy Award, change the way films are made, change Hollywood, or make a whole wad of money—preferably all four. Consequently, those charged with finding scripts would love to have the time to peruse everything that's out there. But it's not possible. Experienced readers who sift through lots and lots of material know that most scripts, while they may be average or even good, even very good, disqualify themselves for various reasons. Maybe they aren't the kind of material the studio's looking for, or the budget may be too big for the reader's company. There can be dozens of reasons why no connection is made.

Don't despair or consider yourself a failure. You've got some other avenues to pursue before you take that job selling insurance. You can hang out at the current "hot" restaurant in town, trying to meet someone who can help. This approach may or may not work. If you try this, remember that you have to keep abreast of the "in" places—they change pretty rapidly in Los Angeles.

There are a couple of other ways to get your scripts noticed.

SHOWCASES

In the past few years, the Internet has sprouted dozens of sites that cater to screenwriters. Several promote writers by carrying the loglines of whatever script the writer wants to sell. This service, naturally, costs money. The sites generally detail how many scripts they've placed into the hands of producers or agents so far.

One such site is *www.inktip.com*. It lists short summaries of screenplays, and you can add your complete screenplay to its pages. It also offers tips and other services for writers.

GET COMPETITIVE

Entering screenplay competitions is another means of getting your script seen. Every year there seem to be more of these competitions springing up, and most are listed on the Net.

Most every screenwriting contest has an online site. For updated and current information, the best thing to do is let Google find the various spots where competitions are listed.

Not all contests are created equal. Some are here today and gone in a couple of years. A Web listing isn't a guarantee of a competition's validity, nor is it a guarantee that promises made by the organizers will be delivered on or even that the delivered promises will be worth anything. Some competitions offer a cash prize and an introduction to an agent. If you win, be sure you insist that the contest coordinator arrange that meeting. With each day that passes after the contest is over, sponsors will be less interested in serving the winner. They will begin the process of organizing the next contest.

The Old School

There are competitions that existed before the Internet and are well established, prestigious, and ongoing. Following are the contests that offer the biggest payouts in terms of money, contacts in the business, and recognition by people in the industry. Unless an 8.0 hits L.A., you probably don't need to check their pedigrees.

The Austin Film Festival Heart of Film Screenplay Competition

General info:
- Two winners each get $3,500

- Agency review of the script

- Work with an established screenwriter to refine material for commercial sale

- Airfare and pass to festival for winners

Contact: Austin Heart of Film Festival
    1604 Nueces
    Austin, TX 78701
    Tel. (800) 310-3378
    www.austinfilmfestival.com
Entry fee: $40 per piece

ABC Entertainment and The Walt Disney Studios Writing Fellowship Program

General info:
- $50,000 to develop your craft at Disney for one year

- All the advantages of working on the Disney lot

- Fifteen full-time participants are selected

- Writing samples are required

- No entry fee

Comments: Well established; competition was begun in 1989
Contact: Writing Fellowship Program
    The Walt Disney Studios
    500 South Buena Vista Street
    Burbank, CA 91521
    Tel. (818) 560-6894
    www.abctalentdevelopment.com

The Nicholl Fellowships in Screenwriting

General info:
- $30,000 paid in five installments over a year

- This contest is so well connected in the business that even the second-tier runners-up get noticed by agents and producers

Comments: This is *the* contest in Los Angeles.
Contact: Nicholl Fellowships in Screenwriting
    1313 North Vine Street
    Los Angeles, CA 90035
    Tel. (310) 247-3101
    www.oscars.org/nicholl
Entry fee: $30 per script

The Sundance Institute

General info:

- Screenwriters Lab: a five-day writers' workshop given twice during the year

- Directors Lab: a three-week workshop for writers and directors with advice from seasoned filmmakers

Comments: This one is bigger and older than the Nicholls. In fact, it's so well established that most of the entrants are seasoned writers.

Contact: Sundance Institute
225 Santa Monica Boulevard, Eighth Floor
Santa Monica, CA 90401
Tel. (310) 394–4662
www.sundance.org

Entry Fee: $30

The Chesterfield Writer's Film Project

General info:

- $20,000 for up to five writers to participate in a year-long program, during which they write two full-length feature film screenplays

Contact: The Chesterfield Writer's Film Project
1158 Twenty-Sixth Street, PMB544
Santa Monica, CA 90403
Tel. (213) 683–3977
www.chesterfield-co.com

Entry Fee: $39.50

Writer's Digest Annual Writing Competition

General info:

- $2,500 grand prize, all categories (fiction, poetry, screenwriting)

- $25 to $1000 for fifth through first place

- $100 worth of *Writer's Digest* books for first through third place

Contact: Writer's Digest Writing Competition
    4700 E. Galbraith Road
    Cincinnati, OH 45236
    Tel. (513) 531–2690
    www.writersdigest.com
Entry fee: $10

If the contest isn't one of the well established, recognized competitions, research it. Call or write to the sponsors to determine how much experience the organizers have running a competition; find out who will be judging, along with their background and experience. Ask what has happened with former winners' works. Be a bit skeptical about any unfamiliar contest you enter, but don't let it keep you from picking and choosing those you think are the best and entering them.

Good luck!

22

Putting the Icing On It

There are other aspects of writing for Hollywood that you'll need to be aware of and learn how to use to aid your pursuit of success as a screenwriter. These have nothing to do with writing, but are ways to give yourself some additional leverage and to help survive with your ego intact in what is considered by all to be a bruising, rude, highly competitive business that too often believes in its own myths rather than in its realities.

THE FLIP SIDE OF WRITING

It's been said a zillion times, and it never changes: Producers and analysts always urge writers who want to succeed to read, read, and read some more. This should include books, screenplays, newspapers, magazines, the classics, just about everything.

KEEPING UP

You need to know who's who and what's what in this business. One way to learn that is to read the trades. You should keep informed of what's going on in the industry.

GET A GRIP

If you're planning to work in this industry and sell more scripts than you can imagine, it is wise to know as much as you can about the process of making movies. As one writer said, "The more understanding you have of the craft, the more you enhance your chance to succeed." You ought to know something about acting, editing, cinematography, and line production. Anything you learn will help you become a knowledgeable professional.

CREATING ILLUSIONS

If you really can't come to Los Angeles, not even briefly, then the next best thing is to create the appearance of living in the city. Whether they admit it or not, when most readers see an out-of-county or out-of-state address on a script, they unconsciously assume the script will be less than professional. This assumption is correct often enough to confirm their fears. If you have a friend who lives in Los Angeles who will accept mail for you, use that friend's address. If you don't know anyone who lives in the area, rent a post office box or private box. Some private box companies use a street address and a suite number instead of a box number. It creates the image of an office or an apartment rather than a postal box.

NETWORKING

Networking is a word that has definitely overstayed its welcome. Yet it's still with us. It's one of those concepts that everyone grabs onto for dear life, as if it's the answer to everything. It isn't. Too often, it creates an image of people trying to meet dozens and dozens of people, not because they like people, enjoy the same career, want to find someone to love or someone to talk to, or want to find others whose passions they share, but because they want to further themselves, i.e., use other people, if they can. I don't think networking plays out that way in reality, yet to hear some people talk, you would think other people are merely stones to step on in their desperate pursuit of success.

Finding others whose company you like and whose interests you share is probably more difficult for writers than it is for performers. Writers' work is isolating and solitary. They don't have to be at the theater at three to rehearse with a half-dozen other people, all of whom they'll learn to like or dislike. In Los Angeles, sidewalk cafés or bars where people are regulars and speak freely to each other and to newcomers are relatively rare. L.A. is a driving city, with people isolated in their cars, not sharing sidewalks. Because they're locked up all day talking to a word processor, lots of writers probably don't have their socializing skills in top form. (Why do you think writers drink? All that aloneness makes you ache for company.) You have to make a point of getting to know people. Lots of people.

Take some classes. Talk to people at the gym, at the supermarket. Join a club, learn to play tennis, get involved in politics. Do stuff that will get you in touch with other people. Take a temporary job at a studio. Do routine clerical or similar work for subcontractors, like optical houses or editing shops or whatever you can find. You'll meet some people. If, like some of the young writers in Los Angeles, you went to UCLA or USC, you've got an advantage. Not only are you friends of and know other ex-students, but lots of people in the industry are alums of those schools.

KEEP IT CURRENT

When you make a contact in this town, keep it. The surprising thing about Hollywood is that you can call someone you haven't spoken to in a couple of years, and usually she'll remember you. That's not necessarily true of agents or professionals, who have huge numbers of people soliciting them, but if you've had a positive face-to-face encounter of more than a minute or two with someone in the business, don't let that contact get away. If someone in the business encourages you, ask him if you can send him other material—and then do it. In all involvements in which you feel there is positive mutual regard, keep in touch.

CLASSY

It is probably a good idea to take some classes in writing and film. Many new writers take classes to improve their writing and to feel like they are part of the scene. The American Film Institute, UCLA, and USC have extensive programs covering all areas of the industry. There are also private classes held by professional industry people.

As you go along in your career, your need for these classes will lessen, but in the early years, they're very helpful. Being around others and talking about writing inspires you to get started on your own projects.

KEEP A LIST

As you learn about the industry, you should pay special attention to those companies that produce the kinds of movies you write. Keep track of them: what they're doing, the new films they have on their production chart, and if someone new comes in as head of production. Keep your finger on their pulse for your own good.

LIFE AS A SCREENWRITER

As a freelance writer, no one is dependent on you to show up to do the job, so it is easy to procrastinate. Here are some tips on how to keep the creative juices flowing.

Getting to Work

If you're writing on spec, it means there is no timeline, and no one is waiting for the pages. You can put off writing until you draw your last breath. Freelance writing takes more discipline than many other professions, at least until someone is willing to pay for your services and you are forced to get yourself going every morning just to meet a deadline.

One way to coerce yourself into writing is to get a partner. When you cowrite, you have to meet with that person and prepare your share of the material. It's a motivating force that's very effective, as long as you get along with your partner, your points of view about material mesh, and each partner is willing to compromise now and again.

More often than not, however, you will write on your own. Many writers swear by having an office or a space away from their home—even if it's the guestroom over the garage. That becomes your work space. If you can't afford to actually rent an office or have a space separate from where you live, you still must arrange an area in your home that is your "office." Set yourself a schedule that's consistent each week; then, every day, get yourself up, get dressed as you would if you were going to an outside job, and arrive at your desk at the appointed time. Work on the projects you are currently writing. If you establish this routine, you'll begin to feel like a writer, even if you haven't sold anything. The ritual itself creates a sense of purpose and belonging.

It's Tough to Do

Writing for the movies is one of the most difficult professions to succeed at. Keep that in mind when the rejection letters and returned scripts start filling your mailbox. All writing jobs are competitive and difficult to get, most are low-paying, and there's little or no net gain in the number of jobs available. For every writing job created in one sector, it seems jobs are lost in another.

Because of the possibility of a high payoff, lots of people are drawn to screenwriting, and that's why it is littered with people who have realized they have to pay to play. Even many experienced people who have already sold scripts have a tough time setting up each subsequent project.

The Check's in the Mail

If you want to be a doctor or a psychiatrist, you know before you start that you won't be hanging out your shingle for probably ten years. You have to spend a lot of time in school and pay a lot of dues. After you get through, you'll probably earn a pretty good living doing something you love. Despite stories to the contrary, being a screenwriter is very similar. It takes a long time to learn the craft, make connections, get through a lot of failed attempts, and survive rejection before your phone starts ringing with offers. Then you'll probably be able to make a pretty good living. Keep in mind that newspapers don't write dog-bites-man stories, they write man-bites-dog stories. The news reports of multimillion-dollar script sales by first-time writers are featured in the trades and entertainment publications because they are the rare man-bites-dog tales.

Sometimes a Screenplay Isn't a Screenplay

There is a saying that suggests, "Luck is being ready when the opportunity presents itself." If you have to sub for the star, it won't be a lucky break if you don't know the dance routine. If you've got a lot of unfinished screenplays lying around, or some unfinished first acts, you don't have a script. And when you meet someone who's looking for the kind of project you've got in your mind but not on paper, and that person says, "Send it," or, "Let me see it," you won't be ready. Being a professional isn't just about talking a good game.

The Hard Part of Writing

Writing isn't all passion and inspiration. Feeling so strongly about something that you have to write about it is passion. That's about 10 percent of the task. The other 90 percent is taking that idea and developing it, working it out, and writing a full, complete story from it. Why do you think successful producers hire writers to work out their movie ideas? Because it's the hard part. If you stop working on a project when the obsession begins to lose its magic, it could mean the difficulty of working out mundane story problems overwhelms you. How will you get anywhere if you're not willing to work something through to the finish—the easy and the hard parts?

Stop for an Hour or Thirty

There are times when you will get blocked. Nothing comes to mind, and what leaks out is seaweed—soggy and shapeless. You can't seem to get anywhere. It's okay. Writer's block happens to everyone somewhere along the line. Don't baby yourself too much. Don't allow yourself to stop just because there's a difficult plot turn coming up. On the other hand, if you're in the middle of that plot turn and suddenly, or slowly, none of the words you write seems to do anything but hang on the page like a smeared fingerprint, stop for a while. Take a break, go bowling, see a movie, do anything to get away from the material. You'll come back to it renewed and ready to begin again. And if you aren't, give it a little more time. You will get started again.

Ego Pumps

You can find ways to make yourself feel bad practically every day in Hollywood. If you aren't hearing the latest success story, you're reading about it. If you aren't getting a rejection, your phone calls aren't answered. If people aren't asking you in so many words when you're going to do something important with your life, they're wondering how insane you are to live without a regular income. Ignore all these taunts. Find your own personal strategies to counteract them. Maybe that will be talking to your best friend or taking a walk on the beach or gardening or imagining all those who make you feel as bad as the target of a dartboard. You've got to keep your spirits up and your goals focused.

Don't Forget Who You Are

As you get more into life as a scriptwriter in Los Angeles, you'll start acting, talking, and thinking like movie people. If this happens, you might lose your own particular vision of the world, and with it will go your ability to create fresh characters and stories. You'll start thinking in terms of stereotypes. You will pursue hipness, hang out at the right places, drive the right-status car, wear the right clothes, support the politically correct causes, and use the current slang. Your personal vision of life, the one you grew up with, the real you, will be gone. If this starts happening, it's time to take a break from Hollywood and recapture your own view of life.

I'm Worth It

It is said that the need to be appreciated is as indigenous to the human character as the need for food and shelter. Taking up the life of a struggling Hollywood writer will earn you very little appreciation of your talents for some time. Until you break through, you will have to suffer rejection and disinterest. Nobody will be around to believe in you, unless you're lucky and come supplied with fans or an adoring spouse. Even then, you will ask yourself, "Do they really love my work, or are they just being kind?" Writing on spec is much easier if you get some positive feedback. Unfortunately, in your position as a struggling writer, very little praise comes your way. You may find it hard to get yourself going every day. The secret is this: You have to believe in yourself absolutely, or you won't make it.

Finally

To keep yourself focused, remember the phrase heard around Hollywood: Every day you don't write, the bastards win.

EPILOGUE

Becoming a screenwriter is an exciting adventure in the truest sense of the word. Like an explorer in the jungle, undertaking such a career requires skill, talent, courage, and perseverance. Like an explorer, you have to blaze your own trail, you live with little safety, and you will make wonderful discoveries.

If in any way this book has been helpful, has provided a few guideposts, then it has done its job.

Here's hoping you find the prize you are searching for in that jungle you're taming. Good luck to you.

KAH

Index

Books from Allworth Press

Allworth Press is an imprint of Allworth Communications, Inc. Selected titles are listed below.

The Best Things Ever Said in the Dark: The Wisest, Wittiest, Most Provocative Quotations from the Movies
by Bruce Adamson (hardcover, 7 ½ × 7 ½, 144 pages, $14.95)

The Screenwriter's Legal Guide, Third Edition
by Stephen F. Breimer (paperback, 6 × 9, 352 pages, $24.95)

Writing Television Comedy
by Jerry Rannow (paperback, 6 × 9, 224 pages, $14.95)

The Screenwriter' Guide to Agents and Managers
by John Scot Lewinski (paperback, 6 × 9, 256 pages, $18.95)

So You Wannabe a Screenwriter: How to Face the Fears and Take the Risks
by Sara Caldwell and Marie-Eve Kielson (paperback, 6 × 9, 240 pages, $14.95)

The Health and Safety Guide for Film, TV and Theater
by Monona Rossol (paperback, 6 × 9, 256 pages, $19.95)

Technical Film and TV for Nontechnical People
by Drew Campbell (paperback, 6 × 9, 256 pages, $19.95)

Jumpstart Your Awesome Film Production Company
by Sara Caldwell (paperback, 6 × 9, 208 pages, $19.95)

Hollywood Dealmaking: Negotiating Talent Agreements
by Dina Appleton and Daniel Yankelevits (paperback, 6 × 9, 256 pages, $19.95)

Creative Careers on Hollywood
by Laurie Scheer (paperback, 6 × 9, 240 pages, $19.95)

An Actor's Guide—Your First Year in Hollywood, Revised Edition
by Michal Saint Nicholas (paperback, 6 × 9, 272 pages, $18.95)

Please write to request our free catalog. To order by credit card, call 1-800-491-2808 or send a check or money order to Allworth Press, 10 East 23rd Street, Suite 510, New York, NY 10010. Include $6 for shipping and handling for the first book ordered and $1 for each additional book. Ten dollars plus $1 for each additional book if ordering from Canada. New York State residents must add sales tax.

To see our complete catalog on the World Wide Web, or to order online, you can find us at ***www.allworth.com.***